BOB OF LYNN

THE FIRST PRIME MINISTER

A HISTORY OF
SIR ROBERT WALPOLE
AND
HOUGHTON HALL

by

CHRIS BOXALL

FOREWORD BY LORD CHOLMONDELEY

Published by Chris Boxall 2008
21, Valley Rise, Dersingham,
King's Lynn, Norfolk, PE31 6PT

ISBN : 978-0-9557786-0-5

Printed by King's Lynn Press, Austin Fields,
King's Lynn, Norfolk, PE30 1PH

DEDICATION

This book is dedicated to the memory of

PERCY BALDWIN

and

EDDIE PEARSON

Two stalwarts of Houghton
who taught me all those things
you won't find in the history books!

FOREWORD

This brief account of the life of Sir Robert Walpole, our first 'Prime Minister', is very welcome, as it concentrates on the private rather than the public man, and gives a much fuller idea of his dealings in Norfolk and of his involvement in the construction and decoration of Houghton Hall than most of the longer biographies.

Chris Boxall has been a guide for the House Opening at Houghton for many years, and his insights into the way the house was built and lived in are based on detailed research and close observation.

'Bob of Lynn' offers a fascinating glimpse into early 18th Century life, and a thoughtful portrayal of one of its most enigmatic characters; it should be of special interest to those who have visited Houghton and want to know more about its history.

David Cholmondeley
Houghton
November 2007

CONTENTS

INTRODUCTION

Many and varied are the books about Sir Robert Walpole, Britain's first Prime Minister. All of them, quite naturally, go into great detail about the great man's political life and career. Several of them, however, tend to promote the political aspects at the cost of the more personal facts and details of his life.

As a keen enthusiast of Walpole and the history of the early Georgian period, I have read many of these biographies and lamented on the absence of information about the man, his family and, especially, his unique relationship with his grand Palladian home, Houghton Hall, in Norfolk.

And so, in writing this brief profile, I have tried to redress the balance in some small way. I have, therefore, deliberately omitted the vast detail of the political career in favour of a more intimate study of Walpole. It is necessary, obviously, to make reference to Walpole the politician from time to time, but not to the same depth of other, more dedicated and academic biographers. This profile is simply intended as an easy and helpful read for the amateur historian, visitor and layman.

For those seeking a more detailed account of Walpole's long and fascinating political career, I would recommend the works of such eminent writers and historians as J.H. Plumb, Brian W. Hill, G.R. Stirling Taylor, John Morley, Harry T. Dickinson, Jeremy Black, Edward Pearce, David Yaxley and many others. A full biography of suitable texts appears at the end of this booklet.
I simply hope to put some flesh on the very ample bones of Sir Robert, in an attempt to bring the man to life for the reader, and to make him more accessible to amateur historians like myself.

He is not currently in vogue, being eclipsed by more famous politicians like Disraeli, Gladstone, Pitt and Churchill. His contribution to history, however, is enormous and one that should not be forgotten.

Walpole was not only Britain's first official Prime Minister, but the longest-serving PM in our history, as well as being one of the first commoners to be made a Knight of the Garter and the first English minister to be given occupancy of 10, Downing Street.

It is only fitting that such a great, though flawed, man should be remembered by history. I only hope I can do him justice.
CHRIS BOXALL
November 2007

Pictured top left: Sir Robert Walpole - J.M. Rysbrack © Houghton Hall
Top right: Sir Robert Walpole - John Wootton © Houghton Hall
Bottom: The Walpole Family - Charles Jervais and John Wootton
l to r: Catherine Walpole, Lord Clinton, Edward Walpole, Robert Walpole (jr), Margaret Rolle, Horace Walpole,
Maria Skerret, Maria Skerret (daughter), Sir Robert Walpole, Charles "Turnip" Townshend, Mary Walpole, Viscount Malpas. © Houghton Hall

West Front of HOUGHTON in NORFOLK.

1
THE SARACEN'S HEAD

In the north-west corner of the county of Norfolk, just below the Lincolnshire border, is a cluster of villages and locations that bear the name of Walpole. They include Walpole St Andrew, Walpole Highway, Walpole Marsh and Walpole St Peter. It was this latter village that gave its name, in Norman times, to the family which would eventually give England its first Prime Minister.

The Walpoles, at this time, were - what they would be for many centuries and generations to follow- a mixture of farmers, landowners, politicians and soldiers. It was in the year 1191 that they would first come to prominence. In that year, King Richard I - 'The Lion Heart' - was conducting the Third Holy Crusade against those in the Middle East he perceived to be heathens in need of conversion to Christianity. The Walpoles were one of several English families helping the monarch to this end.

The main opponents of the Christian Crusaders in the late 12th century were the Saracens, a proud, civilised but fanatical race of Muslim fighters who were led by the charismatic Saladin (Salah-ed-Din Yusuf ibn-Ayyub). In 1191, Richard I was laying siege to the city of Acre, now situated on the coast of northern modern-day Israel. The siege eventually proved successful and the King, as was his custom, rewarded those who had helped him with gifts of money and land, titles and honours. This was how the Walpole family were able to upgrade and move from the Walpole region to new land they had acquired in the area of Houghton, about fifteen miles to the north-east of modern-day King's Lynn. And it was here, at Houghton, that the family built the medieval house that would become the first of the three Houghton Halls to occupy the site. It had formerly been part of Earl Warren's Manor of Rudham.

Houghton took its name from a derivation of two Anglo Saxon words: houge = high, and toune = settlement. It was also known as Houtana or Houtune. Although believed by many to be a flat county, presumably because of its close location to the flatter Fens of southern Lincolnshire, Norfolk does have its fair share of high ground. Houghton stands quite prominently at the top of such a pronounced area overlooking the lower land occupied by such nearby villages as Harpley, Great Massingham, and the Rudhams.

In addition to the King's generosity that allowed the Walpoles to acquire Houghton, the monarch also granted the family the honour of the Saracen's Head. Such an honour was taken very seriously by the Walpoles, who decided to incorporate it into the family coat of arms. This consisted of two chevrons reverse, split by a cross bar on which were placed three cross crosslets. Beneath the crest was the family motto :

'Fari Quae Sentiat', liberally translated from the Latin as "Say What You Feel". This, ironically, some six centuries later, would prove a most suitable and appropriate motto for England's first Prime Minister!

The Walpoles decided to place the Saracen's Head atop the coat of arms but separated by a medieval helmet and visor. There was a slight problem due to the fact that the English medieval painters commissioned to do this decoration had no idea what a Saracen looked like. Through verbal descriptions and simple drawings passed to them by the returning family, they created a strange image of a swarthy-faced man wearing a nightcap-shaped hat and sporting a pointed beard. On most versions, a small wheel can be seen on the hat, in remembrance of Saint Catherine, the legendary Christian martyr of Alexandria, who, in 307 A.D., was tortured on a spiked wheel and beheaded, eventually giving her name to the modern day firework, the Catherine Wheel.

Visitors to Houghton today can see numerous representations of the Saracen's Head all around the Hall and grounds. It appears in various shapes and sizes on ceilings and pediments, furniture and hatchments. At the top of most of the exterior drainpipes, a seemingly darkish blob transforms into a Saracen's Head on closer examination. These images have often prompted enquiries from puzzled visitors about the presence of Mr Punch or a court jester, and children have even asked why Father Christmas should be adorning the ceiling of the Stone Hall!

The Saracen's Head became something of a tradition when it was used as the name for many English public houses. Drive through South Lincolnshire on the A17 and you will even come across a village of that name.

And so the Walpoles had arrived at Houghton, building their first hall and establishing a proud and noble dynasty on the site that would endure for another six hundred years, culminating in two of the family's greatest and most memorable names of the Georgian period – Sir Robert and Horace Walpole.

2
THE COLONEL AND HIS FAMILY

Colonel Robert Walpole was the son of Sir Edward Walpole and his wife, Susan Crane, the daughter and co-heir of Sir Robert Crane of Chilton, Suffolk. Sir Edward had been born at Houghton in 1621, and his wife was nine years his junior. Susan, who would die in her 37th year, was the mother to Sir Edward's twelve children (4 boys and 8 girls), born in a fifteen year period between 1650 and 1665. She would die two years later in 1667.

The first of these offspring was a boy, Robert, born in 1650. Like his father, he would grow up not only to run the Houghton Estate but also to become a Member of Parliament, representing the borough of Castle Rising. He was also a Deputy Lieutenant for the County of Norfolk. In addition, he was also immensely proud of his involvement in the Norfolk Militia, and took both the title of Colonel and his military duties most seriously. In 1671 he would go on to marry 16-year-old Mary, the daughter and heir of Sir Jeffry Burwell* of Rougham, Suffolk. Their happy and devoted alliance would produce a staggering total of nineteen children, in the 23 years between 1672 and 1695. There were to be 11 boys and 8 girls.
The children were:-

Susan	1672	A boy, stillborn	1690
Mary	1673	Charles	1691
Edward	1674	William	1693
Burwell	1675	A girl, stillborn	1695
Robert	1676		
John	1677		
Horatio	1678		
Christopher	1680		
Elizabeth	1681		
Elizabeth	1682		
Galfridus	1684		
Ann	1685		
Dorothy	1686		
Susan	1687		
Mordant	1688		

Some sources also quote Jeffery or Geoffrey

Two of the daughters were both named Elizabeth and there were also to be two Susans. Two other stillborn children were unnamed.

Sadly for the couple, they would lose twelve of these children either at birth or in early infancy due to the high infant mortality rate which prevailed in those times. This was due mainly to the general ignorance of health issues, hygiene and cleanliness that existed at all levels of society, combined with the overall ineptitude of what passed for a medical profession. Such tragic losses, however, were accepted stoically by the parents, for large families and early deaths were part of the normal pattern of life. Only seven of those children would survive to adulthood.

Most of the remaining seven children would go on to make successful careers or enjoy reasonably long lives. The most famous of these would, of course, be Robert, the future and first premier of his country.

Mary would go on to marry Sir Charles Turner of Warham, Norfolk, and they would become the great grandparents of Norfolk's greatest hero, Admiral Horatio Nelson. Mary would die in 1701, some 37 years before her husband, who passed away on 24th November 1738.

Edward would die in 1698. Burwell had already died in 1690 at the Battle of Beachy Head, fought against the French fleet. Horatio married Mary Magdalen, daughter of Peter Lombard, and went on to become his brother Robert's Ambassador to Paris. As boys, the pair were almost inseparable and, in later life, they would be close political allies. It was he who became the 1st Baron Walpole of Wolterton in 1756, and built Wolterton Hall, near Aylsham in Norfolk, the home today of Lord Robin Walpole and his family. Horatio died in 1757.

Galfridus (the Latin for Geoffrey) received a naval commission, went to sea and became a captain in the Navy. He was commanding a ship, the 'Lion', off the Italian coast during the War of Spanish Succession when his vessel was attacked by the French. Three English ships were attacked by five French vessels. The other two English men o'war were able to withdraw, but before he could disengage from the action, Galfridus was to lose his left arm. A portrait of Galfridus, painted by Charles Jervais, now hangs above the fireplace in the Common Parlour at Houghton. He wears a red tunic uniform, for this was in the days before the regulation Navy blue came into effect, and the evidence of his amputation can be clearly seen in the painting. By coincidence, in less than a century later, his great great nephew, Nelson, was also lose an arm in battle. Nelson would eventually inherit Galfridus's silver-hilted sword.

After leaving the Navy, Galfridus went on to become a joint Paymaster-General in 1721 in his brother Robert's government, and married Cornelia, daughter of a James Hays of London. He would die relatively young, at the age of 42, in Greenwich on 5th August 1726, presumably, in some part, as a result of the toll imposed upon him from his earlier war injury.

Dorothy Walpole – known to the family as Dolly - was the apple of her brother Robert's eye. Although no beauty, she was a loving and friendly individual. She would eventually become the second wife of Charles, the 2nd Viscount Townshend (1674-1738), and went to live at nearby Raynham Hall, near Fakenham, Norfolk. It was to be a matter of some vexation for Robert Walpole that Townshend didn't treat Dorothy as kindly as he would have wished.

Townshend, better known as 'Turnip' Townshend and famous for inventing the crop rotation system, would become Walpole's Secretary of State. They enjoyed a long and close friendship until, eventually, Townshend's political and personal jealousies - especially over the newly built Houghton and his treatment of Dorothy - led to an irreparable breach between the two men. Dorothy was to die on 29th March 1726 of smallpox, twelve years before her husband, and was to gain a certain fame and notoriety in her death as part of Norfolk folklore. She is said to be 'The Brown Lady', whose ghost supposedly haunts Raynham Hall, and who, it is claimed, has even been seen further afield at Houghton! This once prompted one old Norfolk wag to comment, "Hev she gotta bike, then?"! After his resignation from the Government in 1729, Lord Townshend was to spend the remainder of his life in seclusion at Raynham. He was known to stand on a mound of high ground at Raynham, gesticulating wildly and swearing in the general direction of Houghton! According to Lord Hervey, George I said of him ... *"there is Townshend, a silent, proud, surly, wrong-headed booby."*

Colonel Robert and Mary Burwell's 14th child, Susan, would marry Anthony Hammond of Wootton, who died in 1743. She would live for a further 20 years as a widow, occupying the south wing at Houghton, before dying in 1763.

Colonel Robert Walpole died on 18th November 1700, on his 50th birthday. His wife, Mary, would survive him by another 11 years. By this time his first two sons, Edward and Burwell, had predeceased him. And so, at the age of 24, it fell to his third son, Robert, to inherit the Houghton Estate and become the new owner of the second Houghton Hall. For the Walpole family, it was to mark the start of a new and exciting era.

3.
THE EARLY YEARS

The fifth child and third son of Colonel Robert and Mary Walpole, young Robert was born in the second Hall, an old manor house at Houghton, on 26th August 1676. It proved to be a difficult birth for Mary, who suffered a long and painful labour. She was attended by the family doctor, Dr. Richard Short, who came from Bury St. Edmunds. The doctor was at Houghton for four days, and was to receive a fee of three guineas for his efforts in delivering the child. Several of Mary's offspring had been sickly, often prone to rickets and fever. Young Robert, however, was to prove to be a fairly healthy, robust and plumpish child, with lively brown eyes.

As a boy, he enjoyed little in the way of luxury, and would wear plain, hard-wearing clothes which were often bought by his father at local fairs or from wandering tinkers. In those early formative years, Houghton and the surrounding area would provide him with those passions which would sustain him for the rest of his life. A love of the outdoors, of hunting and riding and a lifelong devotion to his native county. In later years, when forced to live and work for most of the time in London, he delighted in his all too infrequent visits back to Norfolk and the peace and tranquility of the Houghton estate.

At the age of six, young Robert became a border at the Reverend Richard Ransome's school at Great Dunham, where his brother Edward was already a pupil, and his younger brother, Horatio, would soon follow. He received a thorough elementary education, but there were few holidays for the boy, and he would only return to Houghton two or three times a year, and then only for a week or two. It has also been suggested that, for a short time, the very young Robert may also have been a student at the church school at Great Massingham. During this time away from home, Robert became very close to his brother Horatio, and their companionship helped the boys to deal with the inevitable loneliness they must have experienced.

In 1690, when he was thirteen, Robert was sent to Eton, with the expectation that he would be destined for a church career. In 1696, he went up to King's College, Cambridge, following in the footsteps of his brother Edward and Charles Townshend, and where he would study the classics. Having been away from home for so long, Walpole learned the invaluable lessons of independence, toughness and self assurance which were to stand him in good stead for the future. Life at Cambridge had a profound influence on the young Walpole, although his time there was cut short when, in 1698, he had to return to Houghton to look after his father's estate and learn the business of land and farm management. He later proved his affection for King's by giving the College a payment of £500 in 1723. It is worth noting that J.H. Plumb, in the introduction to his great biography, says that his interest in Walpole was first roused by sitting beneath a picture of the great man hanging over the High Table at King's.

In 1699, the Colonel arranged a marriage between Robert and Catherine Shorter. She was the eldest daughter of John Shorter of Bybrooke in Kent, a timber merchant who traded with the Baltic. Catherine brought with her a dowry of £7000, which was to prove extremely helpful in paying off a number of Walpole mortgages and other debts on the estate. She was a beautiful, slender, round-faced girl with large, full and sensuous lips, and dark, luminous eyes. It is clear to see how the young Robert, who always had an eye for the ladies, was attracted to her, and the sizeable dowry was also a good incentive to their union. She was, however, possessed of a terrible jealousy and outbursts of anger. She had been brought up in London by her grandmother, Lady Phillips, who instilled in her an appetite for fashion and a passion for reckless extravagance. There is no doubt that their early years together were quite passionate, but, eventually, their marriage would suffer the strains of affairs and separations.

During his time at Cambridge, it had been supposed that Walpole was destined for a clerical career. Any hopes of a church living were dashed by Walpole's return home to Houghton, and it was inevitable, therefore, that he would now follow in his father's and grandfather's footsteps by taking up a political career.

The young man had already shown considerable interest in the management of Castle Rising, a small borough on the outskirts of King's Lynn, which his father had represented. With the death of his father, he had to reappraise his future employment. Always an ambitious individual, young Robert knew he needed to do more than just be a Norfolk country squire. And so it was, the following year in 1701, that he entered Parliament as a Whig M.P. for the rotten borough of Castle Rising.

Visitors to Castle Rising today will find a small and beautiful little village nestled around a quaint church, with the ruins of a magnificent Norman castle towering above it. How, they wonder, did such a small and picturesque village manage to return not just one but two M.P.s to Parliament some three centuries ago? The reason is simple. In those days the sea, coming in from The Wash, came up to the site of the present village. This made Castle Rising a very important adjunct to the nearby port and borough of King's Lynn. In the intervening years, land conservation has pushed the sea back, making the area between the village and The Wash rich in agricultural land.

In representing Castle Rising, Walpole was joined by his colleague, Thomas Howard. And so the young member, now in his mid-twenties, went down to London and entered the English Parliament. In those days, it operated out of buildings in Whitehall, the main cut and thrust of debate being done in an area known as the Cockpit. There were two parties – the Whigs and the Tories.

Whig was a name originally applied to Scottish cattle rustlers and horse thieves. The origin of the word is obscure but it is probably a shortened form of "whiggamore", a horse drover. The name was later associated with the Presbyterian Covenanters and later, in the reign of Charles II (1660-1685), to those seeking to exclude the Duke of York from succession to the throne. The name of 'Whig' was used abusively by their Tory opponents. From the time of the Glorious Revolution, the Whigs were upholders of Parliamentary supremacy and toleration for non-conformists. They supported the Hanoverian Succession and enjoyed a monopoly of political power until the reign of King George III, when they were superseded by the Tories after 1783. They did not recover the ascendancy until 1830, the time of the Reform Bill. By 1868, the name Liberal had largely replaced that of Whig. Liberal, as a political term, came to be applied to the more 'advanced' Whigs in the early 19th century.

The name of Tory comes from the Irish – toiridhe or toruidhe, meaning a pursuer or plunderer. The name applied in the 17th century to Irish Roman Catholic outlaws and bandits who harassed the English in Ireland. In the reign of Charles II, the name came to be applied as an abusive term to the supporters of the Crown and its prerogatives at the time of the struggle over the Exclusion Bills. As supporters of the Church of England, they opposed non-conformist and Roman Catholic alike, but most of them acquiesced in the Revolution of 1688.

Tory extremists remained Jacobites at the time of the Hanoverian Succession, which led to a Whig monopoly of political power during the reigns of George I and George II. They resumed office under William Pitt the Younger, and remained dominant throughout the period of the French Revolutionary and Napoleonic Wars. From about 1830, the Tory Party, under the leadership of Sir Robert Peel, came to be called Conservative, the older name having become associated with reaction.

From the very beginning of his political career, Robert Walpole relished Parliamentary life, proving himself to be a willing learner, a capable workhorse and a first class debater. At first he was greeted, in some quarters, with a certain amount of derision from the more aristocratic and snobbish members of London society. He was, after all, something of a country bumpkin in their eyes. Fairly corpulent, with a ruddy complexion and a thick Norfolk accent, he was seen to be something of a Parliamentary yokel and everything a country squire should be. But he had, and always would have, a very thick skin when it came to what people thought of him. In fact, he was able to turn the tables on many of his critics and scorners, who would soon learn, to their chagrin, that Walpole could easily play the bumpkin and yokel when it suited him to do so, and then, having fooled them, defeat them completely. But Walpole was also being noticed and appreciated by those who mattered, and it wouldn't be long before he held government office.

Despite being somewhat short and dumpy, possessed of a florid complexion and with a tendency for wearing somewhat grubby clothes, Walpole was, nevertheless, an imposing individual and could dominate by his sheer weight, presence and confidence. Although coarse in his speech, outspoken and possessing that strong Norfolk accent which he was never to lose, Walpole would become one of the great debaters and orators of his time, and could hold an audience with the powers of that considerable oratory. In 1720, at the time of the great South Sea Bubble debacle, it was Walpole's speech to the House that would help to save the country from ruin. He had developed the habit of staying awake during the longer and more tedious debates in the House of Commons by munching on large numbers of Norfolk apples.

After about a year, in 1702, Walpole was now persuaded by family and friends to go for the bigger prize, and became the Member of Parliament for the borough and port of King's Lynn, the centre of east coast trading with the Continent. He would continue to represent the borough for the next forty years, becoming, in the main, a popular and well liked and well trusted politician. Such was his popularity in many quarters that the people of the town, not renowned for standing on ceremony, simply called him 'Bob of Lynn'. For all the titles and accolades that would be heaped on him throughout his life, this probably meant more to Walpole than most!

Walpole would live through the lives of six monarchs, beginning with Charles II and James II, and would work under four of them – William III and Mary, Queen Anne, George I and George II. It was under the last two that he would do his greatest work and achieve his most outstanding successes.

Queen Anne came to the throne in 1702, and most of her twelve year reign was to be blighted by the protracted and costly War of Spanish Succession, a conflict involving England, the Netherlands and some German states against Spain, France, Portugal and their allies. The great battles of Blenheim, Ramilles, Oudenaarde and Malplaquet – waged and won by his very good friend, John Churchill, 1st Duke of Marlborough – were a clear indicator to the young and ambitious Walpole of how not to conduct a government. Even then, Walpole had little doubt that he would eventually become a senior politician in a position of power. It was just a matter of time.

He put his initial step onto that great ladder when, in June 1705, he entered government for the first time as a member of Prince George's Admiralty Council. If not the most illustrious of positions, it was, nevertheless, a start.

Anne, who gave her support to the Tories, was not pleased with a Whig victory in the General Election of 1708. Walpole, however, saw it as a most positive sign for possible advancement. The Whigs' success was to be short lived when their ministry was overturned in 1710.

In 1708 Walpole was made Secretary at War, and, by 1710, had also become Treasurer of the Navy. He was most certainly a product of his political age. To understand the man, it must be appreciated that, in addition to being a most capable, hard working and proficient politician and, later, a great statesman, he was also terribly ambitious, vain and corrupt. But this was the age of corruption, and Walpole should not be singled out for being unique in this field. It was just that, by virtue of his position, power and expertise, he simply became better at the game than most!

As a result of his activities as Secretary at War, he found himself under attack from his rivals in the Tory party. Censured on 17th January 1712, he was accused of corruption over a forage contract involving the food for army horses in Scotland. It was claimed he had reserved a share of the contract for the personal benefit of his friend, banker and confidential agent, Mr Robert Mann. Walpole, naturally enough, denied the accusation but was expelled from the Commons, arrested and put into the Tower of London, while further enquiries were made into the affair. Unlike many previous occupants of the Tower, his incarceration was not a totally unhappy affair. Although imprisoned, he was not manacled or subjected to any major discomfort, and friends were allowed to visit him with hampers of food and news of Parliamentary affairs.

He found his confinement to be part annoyance and part amusement. Despite all his faults, he was an extremely good and dedicated politician and took his work very seriously. The annoyance came from the fact that he was being prevented from continuing with this work. The amusement came from the fact that he knew his enemies would not be able to prove anything against him. And so it was. By the end of that Parliamentary session in July 1712, nothing had been discovered and the authorities were forced to release him. It might be thought that such suspicions and accusations would have ruined, or, at least, hampered his career. Far from it. His career blossomed. He was only 35-years-old, and, within ten years, he was to become the most powerful politician in England.

4.
THE RISE TO POWER

Queen Anne was in poor health, and her Tories were in disarray, being split between those who supported the Jacobites and others who were for the Hanoverian Succession, while many others in the party were trying to remain neutral. The War of Spanish Succession had finally ended, and the terms of the Treaty of Utrecht in 1713 confirmed Louis XIV of France's belief that the war had been all about trade. Under the terms of the Treaty, England gained Gibraltar, Minorca, Newfoundland and Nova Scotia. Belgium, Milan and Naples were ceded to Austria. Robert Walpole wasted no time in criticising the treaty in a pamphlet entitled "A Short History of Parliament".

The Queen died on 1st August 1714, and the Whigs ensured the peaceful succession of King George I, thus securing the rule of the Hanoverians over any possible Jacobite and Catholic monarchy. Walpole was one of those at the forefront of the Hanoverian victory and his star was once more in the ascendancy. From 1714 to 1717 he was made Paymaster-General, and he enjoyed office as First Lord of the Treasury and Chancellor of the Exchequer from 1715-17. Walpole was now getting his first taste of real power.

The Whigs were not to have things all their own way, however. George I, a somewhat truculent and stupid monarch, wasn't quite as pliable as the new government had hoped. Refusing to speak English and more concerned with his beloved Hanover than with England and its affairs, he would rather listen to his German ministers and German mistresses before he would ever consider dealing with an English minister.

By now Walpole had seen off his most deadly of political enemies, Henry St John Bolingbroke, a Tory and closet Catholic who had negotiated the Treaty of Utrecht. Bolingbroke had been exposed in an attempt to restore the 'Old Pretender', James Francis Edward Stuart, to the throne and was forced to flee abroad, where he served as an adviser at the French court and dreamed of getting his revenge on his great adversary.

Although few Tories would actually take part in the abortive Jacobite rebellion of 1715, the Tories were now damned in the eyes of the King. George, however, was still anxious for an alliance with France in order to preserve the interests of Hanover.

Despite being Paymaster-General, Walpole had little influence with government policy. It was a lucrative post, however, and he had control of a great deal of patronage. He was in a position to achieve his main aims – power and wealth. And his very good friend Townshend was also riding high as a Secretary of State. But things were about to change.

Walpole would incur the King's displeasure when he refused to pay for German mercenaries.

Meanwhile, the Prince of Wales, always at odds with his father, was conspiring with some discontented Whigs to improve his lot with regard to his political influence and remuneration.

Lord Sunderland - made Lord Lieutenant of Ireland and then Lord Privy Seal by George I – was jealous of the more important offices held by his rivals, Walpole and Townshend. With the assistance of Lord Stanhope, he set about convincing others that Walpole and Townshend were actively encouraging the Prince of Wales in his rebellion against his father. Townshend, having been made the new Lord Lieutenant of Ireland, was dismissed from his office in April 1717.

Walpole, along with some other loyal Whigs, resigned his posts and followed his good friend into opposition. Determined to regain power at the earliest opportunity, Walpole happily abandoned some of his Whig principles and pursued a policy of outright opposition to the government at every available opportunity. As a result, he became an extremely effective opposition leader. Realising that power was shared between the Court and the Commons, he began a programme of ingratiating himself with the Royals. He promised to help the King in a proposal to pay off debts on the Civil List; put himself on good terms with the Duchess of Kendal, the King's favourite mistress; and used his influence on the Prince by persuading the latter to submit to the King.

Walpole, however, was still far from his desired seat of power. But, yet again, events were taking place which would soon rectify this situation. The Bubble was about to burst.

Pictured top left: Site of the old village of Houghton. Author's Collection.
Top right: Water Tower, Houghton. Author's Collection.
Bottom: East Front, Houghton Hall. © Houghton hall.

5
THE SOUTH SEA BUBBLE

The National Debt – the total outstanding public borrowings of the central government secured on the national revenue – was first established in a permanent form in the early 1690s, during the reign of William III. It has been managed by the Bank of England since 1750.

By 1710, the National Debt was in the region of £9 million and rising. Robert Harley, as Chancellor of the Exchequer, was finding it increasingly difficult to balance the books.

At this point, the aptly named John Blunt appeared on the scene. It was a case of Blunt by name, blunt by nature. A fat and pompous business man, he was an ambitious individual with a thirst for power and a desire to be rich at any price. Totally without scruples, he had the skills to connive, flatter, cajole and ingratiate himself with those he saw as being able to fulfil his ambitions. This description, by coincidence, would also have fitted Robert Walpole admirably!

Blunt was involved with the Sword Blade Company, an enterprise set up to import the fine, sophisticated and better crafted French sword blades into England, in an attempt to replace the commoner and coarser type of English rapier that was normally used by the gentry. Not content with the import of swords, Blunt and his fellow directors saw a way to improve their financial status by setting themselves up as a banking institution and, in the process, daring to rival the long established Bank of England. The newly formed Sword Blade Bank went so far as to offer the Government a loan of £1.5 million.

Before long, Blunt was in talks with Harley to raise funds by means of a lottery. The Sword Blade Bank would operate the scheme, which was to prove quite popular and fruitful for all those concerned with it. Blunt and his directors now decided to go a step further, and, on 10th September 1711, they formed an offshoot of the Sword Blade Bank which was intended to trade with markets opening up in South America. This newly formed enterprise was to be called the South Sea Company, and Robert Harley was persuaded to become its Governor. Blunt, ever the opportunist, continued to ingratiate himself with those in power and high office, and even went so far as to win over King George I.

The new South Sea Company began trading out of its offices in Threadneedle Street and a couple of less-than-successful expeditions to South American waters were mounted. But any thoughts of serious trading for profit were soon neglected in favour of more profitable money-making schemes at home.

In 1717, Walpole, as Chancellor of the Exchequer, had established the Sinking Fund, the name given to a Government fund, the interest from which was intended to 'sink' or pay off the National Debt.

But, by 1720, the National Debt, now under the control of a new chancellor, John Aislabie, stood at an alarming and staggering £31 million. The cost of the War of Spanish Succession (1701-1714) and the subsequent financial demands of the Army and Navy had pushed the Government's borrowing requirements steadily higher with each passing year. The demands of the ever-rising Civil List for the Royal Household and other financial commitments had also helped to swell the debt to such horrendous proportions.

The South Sea Company now made the very bold offer to the Government of taking over the whole of the National Debt, including loans which had been subscribed by the Bank of England and the East India Company. This proposal, not surprisingly, received strong resistance and objection from the Bank of England. The South Sea Company offered over £7 million to take over the National Debt, and agreed to accept an interest rate on this stock of 5% up to 1727, and 4% thereafter.

Once shares of South Sea stock were issued, the demand for them exceeded all expectations. People from all walks of life were anxious to be involved in the scheme, which offered the promise of great rewards. The cost of the shares grew rapidly, and the market was in a frenzy as the original £100 shares were eventually selling for as much as £1,000, and reaching their highest point at £1,050. When the public demanded far more shares, the company, under Blunt's direction, happily obliged by printing and issuing more without having the collateral to back them up. It was an impossible situation that was ripe for disaster.

Meanwhile, Robert Walpole had now been made Paymaster General again. Although it was but a minor role, he was back in government, if not in the Cabinet, and he was certainly not among the favourites at Court. His good friend Townshend had been appointed Lord President of the Council.

Walpole, who had many friends among the Directors of the Bank of England, was critical of the South Sea Company's actions and had agreed to put the Bank's case before the Commons. He was not, however, totally against the fundamentals of the South Sea scheme.

Realising there was a chance to make a large fortune out of it, he began investing heavily in South Sea shares himself, selling them at a handsome profit, and then promptly reinvesting again. On one occasion he sold £18,000 worth of shares for over £24,000, which was something of a mystery because, at that particular time, he only possessed stock to the value of £9,760. He also managed to secure South Sea stock for the Prince and Princess of Wales.

The same wild speculation which had gripped the nation also held Walpole firmly in its grasp. And, as many others would do, he was in the running for making a terrible loss, had it not been for the timely intervention of a man called Robert Jacombe. Walpole's bank account was with the firm of Messrs Gibson, Jacob and Jacombe of Lothbury Street, London. Robert Jacombe, as well as being the Under Secretary-at-War, was also Walpole's personal banker.

By now, encouraged by the early successes of the South Sea Company, many others were launching all manner of fraudulent and impractical companies and schemes. The Government, encouraged and supported by a biased South Sea Company, passed the Bubble Act which was intended to prevent the establishment of such enterprises. But the price of South Sea stock had suddenly started to slump, and the Company was in trouble.

With the intuitive knowledge of a banker, Jacombe could see what was going to happen and warned Walpole to sell his shares and extricate himself from any further involvement with the scheme. But Walpole, normally astute and careful in such matters, was initially reluctant to heed his banker's advice and was determined to keep on trading. But Jacombe was insistent, and Walpole finally conceded.

It has been suggested that Walpole never actually profited by his dabbling in South Sea shares. Admittedly, by pulling out of the scheme, he was forced to cut his losses, but he had certainly made a healthy profit in his various tradings. His only regret was that he couldn't have made more.

With the South Sea Company now in the early stages of a financial meltdown, Walpole approached the Bank of England and persuaded it to bail out the South Sea Company by offering to buy its stock at £400 for £100. But as the market price fell below this sum, the Bank got cold feet and promptly backed out of their agreement.

Walpole removed himself from the capital and wisely returned to the peace and tranquility of Houghton. By doing so, he had clearly divorced himself from any criticisms or accusations that might have been levelled at him. He also had other concerns to worry about, as his beloved daughter Catherine, always in poor health, was now desperately ill.

And then, inevitably and just as Jacombe had anticipated it would, the Bubble burst. Blunt's ambitious and fraudulent share flotation had finally run out of steam and overreached itself. The shares of the South Sea Company were worthless.

London was now in an uproar and the tentacles of panic quickly reached to all corners of the country. Many investors realised they had been cruelly duped, and that, in many instances, they were now destitute. Lives were ruined, estates lost, families forced into poverty and, in several cases, some of those who had suffered saw no alternative but to commit suicide.

Up at Houghton, just over a hundred miles from the capital, Walpole was far from idle. He was fully aware of what was going on. Jacombe, acting as his eyes and ears, was keeping him well informed of events. No sooner had Walpole returned to Norfolk than his name was on everyone's lips. Jacombe wrote to him saying, *"They all cry out for you to help them!"* This must have done wonders for Walpole's ego. Nevertheless, he decided to bide his time and waited at the old manor house at Houghton. The city needed to suffer a little longer until he was ready to step into the breach.

Nor had Jacombe been idle. He had helped to devise a solution to the problem which he put to his esteemed client. His answer, in simple terms, was to divide the South Sea Company's capital and its debt between the Bank of England and the East India Company.

Walpole decided the time for waiting was over. He ordered his carriage to be prepared, returned to London and began to convince his colleagues and political associates of the wisdom of Jacombe's scheme. They, in turn, set about convincing others, and, as a result, Walpole's efforts to re-establish public credit and his own popularity – and with it his absolute power – proved successful.

Despite his earlier dealings in South Sea stock, he had, by his sojourn to Houghton, disassociated himself from any involvement with the Company. Some believed him to be in the pay of the Bank of England, and he knew that some ministers were against his ideas. In particular, Stanhope and Sunderland were reluctant to let Walpole take any part in the affair when Parliament was recalled on 8th December 1720 to debate the matter. Sunderland, it appears, relented in the hope that it would ruin Walpole once and for all.

Walpole, however, having negotiated with the Bank and the companies, entered the House with the clear and certain knowledge that he would win. He put Jacombe's proposals before Parliament and, using the full power of his amazing oratory, received the almost unanimous backing of the House. In so doing, he had helped to stop the rot and quell the panic, put the country back on the road to fiscal recovery, won the general support of the public, secured confidence in the Government and the Treasury, and, more importantly, insured his own unassailable popularity and certain return to power.

Once the panic had began to subside, the public were soon clamouring for revenge and retribution on those in the South Sea Company who had allowed the debacle to happen. But it wasn't just the directors of the company who were to blame. The duplicity and corruption had reached high into the ranks of the Government, and members of the Royal Household were also implicated.

Realising just what was at stake if so many high ranking ministers and officials were denounced, Walpole set about playing down the scandal. There was to be an enquiry and several of the Company's directors who sat in the House were expelled, sent to the Tower, and had their estates sequestered for the use of the unfortunate investors.

John Aislabie, as Chancellor of the Exchequer, was accused of corruption, saw fit to resign his post and was duly sent to the Tower. Charles Stanhope, Secretary of the Treasury, was also charged with corruption but survived a Committee vote against him by three votes, and was compelled to resign.

Scapegoats were needed and vengeance was partially satisfied when three of those involved in the scandal died. Charles Stanhope's cousin, James Stanhope, died of apoplexy while speaking in the House of Lords. James Craggs Snr committed suicide rather than face conviction and financial ruin. And his son, James Craggs Jnr, Secretary of State, died of smallpox.

Attention now turned to the Earl of Sunderland, as First Lord of the Treasury. He was, without doubt, Walpole's most dangerous and powerful enemy within the ranks of the Whig party. It was imperative for Walpole to crush him if he could, but he was powerless to do so because of Sunderland's popularity with the King and both the King's mistresses – the Frauleins von Schulenberg and Kielmannsegge.

The Commons held a debate to determine Sunderland's guilt. Walpole, despite his feelings towards his old adversary, acted in his defence, ably assisted by his protege, Henry Pelham. It was essential that Walpole retained the confidence of the Whigs and the King. Sunderland was duly acquitted by 233 votes to 172. He eventually resigned his post at the Treasury, although he retained several of his other offices, including that of Groom of the Stole, and control of the Secret Service funds.

Considering the magnitude of his involvement in the scandal, John Blunt escaped relatively lightly. By co-operating with the enquiry and naming names, he was stripped of his assets, being initially allowed a mere £1,000 to live on. This was eventually increased to £5,000, and he quite rightly thought it prudent to retire, albeit in disgrace, to Bath.

Another complication in pursuing or prosecuting those involved in the scandal came when Robert Knight, the Cashier of the South Sea Company, decided to flee to the Netherlands after two very gruelling sessions of cross examination by the investigating committee. In his flight, he also took with him several of the Company's incriminating documents and the notorious green book. This was a ledger which showed falsified accounts and named all those in high places who had enjoyed shady and corrupt dealings with Blunt and his directors.

Walpole realised just how ruinous the revelations of this would be should its contents ever be made public. Orders were given to pursue Knight, who was duly caught and imprisoned. But further orders were issued and he was mysteriously allowed to escape into exile when a hole was conveniently blasted in his prison cell wall! The green book and the other incriminating documents disappeared and were never seen again.

For his actions in covering up the dealings of many who were involved in the scandal, Walpole earned himself a new and uncomplimentary nickname – Skreen-Master General, or the Skreen.

On 3rd April 1721, Robert Walpole was appointed Chancellor of the Exchequer and First Lord of the Treasury. This now made him the most powerful politician in the country. His friend, Charles Townshend succeeded Charles Stanhope, and returned to his former post as Secretary of State.

Walpole now earned himself yet another new nickname. Intended as an insult and a slur on his character, he was now referred to as the 'Prime (or First) Minister'. The phrase quickly came into common usage and was generally accepted by the public as the new title for Walpole's high office. Walpole, although fully aware of the new term, declined to use it himself.

Thus was history born. Robert Walpole became the first Prime Minister of England, and would go on to be the country's longest serving incumbent of this office. He would serve a total of 21 years in the post, from 1721 to 1742. But, to be totally correct, he would actually remain in office for 20 years and 314 days.

On the strength of his handling of the South Sea Bubble crisis, Walpole had finally achieved his ambition of absolute power.

But how sad it is that very few, if any, now remember Robert Jacombe, the man who helped to make that long and illustrious premiership possible.

6
THE PRIME MINISTER

It is a sad fact of today's life that Sir Robert Walpole and his times have been, in the main, woefully overlooked by the public in general. He and his period have been, in some instances, neatly airbrushed from the school curriculum, depriving many children the chance of learning about a rich and fascinating vein of British political and social history. The average response to any enquiry about Walpole will usually result in providing a mere three basic facts about the man. That he was the first Prime Minister, had some involvement in the South Sea Bubble and was also corrupt.

He lived through a wonderful age of achievement in many fields. His was a time of great development in so many areas of English life. Inigo Jones was stunning the world with his architectural style. William Kent dazzled the eye with his masterly designs. Christopher Wren, with his magnificent creation, St Paul's, had placed a building of tremendous passion and breathtaking beauty on the new London skyline following the horrendous conflagration which had earlier engulfed the City in 1666.

The arts were also well represented. Hogarth captured the spirit of the age with his canvasses and drawings, showing both the richness of society and the poverty of Gin Lane. Handel impressed with his amazing music, composing such masterpieces as his 'Water Music' and 'The Messiah'. And writers like Henry Fielding, John Gay, Jonathan Swift and Alexander Pope - many of whom would also be the bane of Walpole's life – brought a new and exciting dimension to English literature. The list of great achievers, innovators and talents seemed almost endless.

This was also the age of grace and grandeur, scandal and corruption. Those with title and position lived life on a grand scale, where money, power, the acquisition of land and the building of great mansions was accepted as the norm. It was the age of the Court, where the monarchy literally reigned supreme, setting the fashion and the style of the times. For those with influence, wealth and standing it was an age of balls, soirées, picnics and parades. A time to be seen and admired, to flirt, seduce and outrage. It was the era of the fop, the beau, the rake, the dandy, the mistress and the courtesan.

But while society ruled, life at the other end of the spectrum was far from easy. Poverty was rife, and disease, often spread by vermin, rampant. The poor drowned their sorrows with gin as they lived in vile and filthy conditions, and any thoughts of health care and welfare were practically non-existent. Open sewers ran through streets and effluent poured continually into the fleets and rivers. The River Thames, London's vital trading highway, was so badly polluted that it became known as 'The Great Stink'.

Crime was also rife, with hanging still being the normal and acceptable punishment for even the most petty of misdemeanours. Children could be hanged for stealing a loaf of bread. Beggars - often the neglected victims of military campaigns – tried to eke out a miserable living in a heaving world of street hawkers, prostitutes and roving bands of cut-throats.

And, somewhere in between, there was a middle class of hard-working but still fairly impoverished tradesmen, servants, grooms, midwives, craftsmen and many others who strived to escape the gutter or the poorhouse and aim for a better and more prosperous life. For many men, despite its hardships and the ever-present risk of death or disfigurement, a life in the Army or the Navy was preferable to starving.

And life in the country, although healthier to some extent, was still hard for the poor and working classes. Long hours working in the fields for pitiful wages, a lack of respect from those who hired them and little hope of advancement made for generally intolerable conditions. And servants, toiling in the grand houses, also worked long days under hard and harsh conditions.

This was not an age of welfare reform and technological advance. The Industrial Revolution was still well over a hundred years away. Life expectancy was short, with most people dying long before they reached the age of fifty. Infant mortality was high, and stillbirths a common event. Medical research was still in its infancy. There were those who had a grounding in basic anatomy and the most brutal of surgical techniques, but a knowledge of serious and effective medicines was a long way off in an age that still relied on dubious pills, doubtful potions, quack tonics and natural remedies in their crudest form.

This was the age of Robert Walpole, and one on which he would place his mark with a firm hand. His two major passions - the lust for power and the love of money – went hand-in-hand. A great deal has been made about his corruption, but this was also the age of corruption. It was rife in all walks of life and at all levels to some degree. Not even the church or the law were exempt. It was a time of bribes, backhanders, sinecures, rotten boroughs, rigged elections, fraud and patronage. We have already seen how someone as unscrupulous as John Blunt could go so far as to deceive a whole nation. That Walpole should be the only one remembered today for his corruption is, perhaps, a little unfair, but it is due to the fact that he was in the highest position possible to do so, and that he did it with such skill and aplomb, and certainly without any degree of conscience.

From the start of his Premiership, he had two clear aims. The first was to conduct a successful foreign policy, and the second was to raise as much revenue for the Government as possible.

His foreign policy was divided into two parts – to keep the peace with other nations, especially England's two main enemies, France and Spain, and to encourage trade with all those nations within reach of

England's ships. Successful trade with its imports and exports would bring much needed revenue into the Treasury coffers. How ironic, therefore, that the country's first and longest serving Prime Minister would never actually leave these shores and go abroad. This seems almost inconceivable to us now in a time when ministers, presidents and other heads of state are constantly attending conferences all around the world!

In attempting to keep the country at peace, Walpole also realised that, apart from the beneficial effects of such action, it would also help to keep the Government's financial reserves intact. He had seen how the War of the Spanish Succession, although successfully fought by Marlborough and others, had been ruinous in terms of cash flow. Men had to be fed, clothed, equipped and transported abroad. Horses had to be purchased and forage constantly provided. The Navy required fast and efficient ships, along with the crews and provisions to man them. And war meant casualties, pensions and medical provisions.

When he had been Paymaster, Walpole had been in virtual control of Chelsea Hospital, a post which, in addition to its good endeavours, had also earned Walpole a comfortable living. He had been so delighted with the little house and garden at the back of the Hospital that he managed to retain control of it even after relinquishing his post as Paymaster. He also got John Vanbrugh to improve the dwelling, known as Orford House, and it would become his chief London residence for the rest of his life, although he maintained other residences at various times in Dover and Arlington Streets. Walpole also added some nine and a half acres of land to the hospital grounds and turned it into a splendid garden at the Hospital's expense. He made his old schoolfriend, the Rev Henry Bland, parson of Great Bircham in Norfolk, Chaplain; brought in his Norfolk doctor, Mr Hepburn, as Surgeon's mate; and allowed his friend, the M.P. Henry Parsons, to become Purveyor. Parsons had happily repaid Walpole's kindness by selling him the Hospital's victualling bills at a handsome 5% discount.

Despite his efforts to save the country from war, Walpole still had to set money aside to maintain a large standing army, the threat of war being ever present. His desire to keep England in a state of peace would enable him to proudly boast in 1734 to Queen Caroline : *"Madam, there are fifty thousand men slain this year in Europe, and not one Englishman."*

Such were his efforts that he skilfully managed to avoid war until 1739.

In his attempts to raise essential revenue, he introduced a new excise scheme, and brought in a raft of new and unpopular taxes on such items as candles, salt, malt and beer. He did, however, abolish old import and export duties on coffee, tea, cocoa, wines and tobacco, but levied an inland or excise duty when these goods were sold for domestic consumption. He gave greater powers to the Customs and Excise to enforce the payment of duty, making him extremely unpopular with a nation of coastal smugglers. The imposition of such duties, revenues and taxes led to inevitable protests and occasional riots, and Walpole would later have to revise, modify and even abolish some of these taxes. These measures, however, were bringing in about £120,000 per annum to the Treasury. And Walpole, ever the opportunist, saw no harm from time to time in happily accepting smuggled brandy, claret, burgundy and champagne!

It is to Walpole's credit that over his 21 years in power he was able to redeem the National Debt to the tune of some £12.5 million.

With clear and rational objectives, expedient and pragmatic policies and methods that were generally effective if often suspect, he was able to dominate a successful administration. He was able to achieve all his main political aims, and was able to command the support of the Monarchy as well as the general confidence of Parliament.

Walpole had always been a supporter of the Glorious Revolution and the Hanoverian Succession. In supporting the arrival of William III to our shores and the reign of Queen Anne, he had managed to establish his desire to keep the nation free of a Catholic monarchy. This was enhanced by the subsequent arrivals to the throne of George I and George II.

Throughout Walpole's term in office, there would be several plots to re-establish a Catholic monarch to the throne of England. Some of these plots were, to say the least, quite poorly planned and thought out. The Government was able to call upon the services of a reasonably efficient intelligence service to root out and arrest a number of plotters. They were also aided in their task by those who were only too willing to act as informers for a variety of reasons, the most common being reward or revenge.

When he was in his late thirties, Walpole had witnessed the furore caused by the ill-fated 1715 Rebellion. This had been an attempt by James Edward Stuart, the only son of James II, to lead a Jacobite rebellion. He had landed at Peterhead in 1715, but his stay in Scotland had been short lived and he left a few weeks later to spend the majority of his remaining fifty years living in Rome. Stuart, also known as The Old Pretender, had, for a brief period, caused some concern to the English government during its honeymoon period with George I in the first year of his reign.

Walpole had made it a personal crusade to prevent such an occurrence again. No sooner had he become Prime Minister, than he was faced with one of the most famous of the Jacobite plots. Called the Atterbury Plot, it took its name from the ambitious Bishop of Rochester who had plotted a Jacobite overthrow of the monarchy. It was an inept exercise on the part of the plotters, most of whom were quickly rounded up. No evidence could be found to actually implicate Bishop Atterbury, who escaped with his life but was duly banished. Several other plotters were sent to prison for their part in the plot. A Norfolk lawyer, Christopher

Layer, was not so lucky. He had made the drastic mistake of leaving a written account of his actions and, for this, he was executed.

Whilst trying to keep a Catholic monarchy at bay, Walpole now had the unenviable job of keeping his new Hanoverian king happy.

George I would present something of a challenge to Walpole by refusing to speak English to his chief minister. Walpole got around this little difficulty by conversing with the King in Latin. He also relied on Robethon, a Hanoverian diplomat, to act as an interpreter with the King. George I was quite happy to be an English king just as long as he didn't have to worry about the throne. He was never happier than when he was with his mistresses or could return to his native Hanover. Nothing could prove better for Walpole who had a clear field in which to operate without any major Royal interference.

Walpole's influence and success with the King was clearly illustrated when, in 1725, he was made a Knight of the Bath. An even greater honour came the following year when he became one of the first commoners to be appointed a Knight of the Garter, without doubt the greatest honour he ever achieved. Such was his pleasure at receiving this title that he would emblazon his new Hall at Houghton with numerous references to the Garter, incorporating them into the furniture and ceiling designs.

So proud was he of receiving the Garter, that he even went so far as to paint the honour into portraits of himself which had been painted prior to 1726. His vanity earned him the nickname of 'Sir Blue String', and contemporary ballads portrayed him as an object of ridicule:-

"In body gross, of Saffron Hue,
Deck'd forth in Green with Ribband Blue."

Life under George II was not quite so easy. No sooner had the King come to the throne in June 1727, than he dismissed Lord Malpas, Walpole's son-in-law, as Master of the Robes. Walpole promptly responded by putting Malpas into the Admiralty.

The King, unlike his father, could speak English and was notoriously stubborn. He was also possessed, at times, of an abominable temper, probably exacerbated by the painful piles from which he suffered on a regular basis. He disliked all things English in preference for all things German and Hanoverian. Walpole knew that negotiating with the King would not always be an easy matter. And so he devised a cunning technique to achieve his needs.

If Walpole had a good idea, he would float it past Queen Caroline at their regular Monday evening meetings at her quarters in the Royal Household.

The Queen was of similar opinions as the King, but, being more prudent and sensible than her husband, tended to keep her thoughts to herself. She was well educated, being learned in ancient and modern history, had a good memory and took an interest in metaphysics, speculating on the nature of being, truth and knowledge. She also had the reputation of being a little heterodox in her notions. She referred to Walpole as 'Le Gros Homme'.

Having been appraised of Walpole's ideas, she would, at a convenient and suitable point, run them past His Majesty. He, in turn, would see the merit of such ideas, implement them and claim the credit. He was happy. Walpole, needless to say, was also happy, having achieved what he had planned all along.

But the happiest of the trio was Queen Caroline. On top of the King's Civil List of some £900,000, Walpole arranged for Caroline to receive a personal allowance of £100,000, plus the use of Somerset House and Richmond Lodge. Needless to say, when Queen Caroline died in great pain after a terrible illness on the Sunday night of 20th November 1737, Walpole was to lose a very good friend and ally.

After the initial suspicions of each other at the beginning of the reign, George II and Walpole became fairly good friends, with Walpole often acting as a negotiator in the constant conflict between the King and the Prince of Wales. The King and Queen were close enough to Walpole to eventually act as the 'sponsors' or godparents to his grandson George, presenting Walpole with a beautiful child's bed which is still on display at Houghton Hall to this day. For a Minister to get this close to the Royal personages speaks volumes about Walpole's power and personality.

The King had also shown his gratitude to his first minister by presenting him with 10, Downing Street, which Walpole gratefully accepted for his office as First Lord of the Treasury. The property had originally been given by George I to Baron Johann Caspar Von Bothmar, the Hanoverian Minister in London.

Walpole also achieved a great deal of domestic harmony despite some of his harsher measures. A country enjoying a long period of peace and reasonable prosperity can usually accept and forgive their leader almost anything if not always agreeing with him.

But, of course, he had his enemies. The most aggressive of these had been the disgraced and exiled Henry St. John Bolingbroke. But there were others in the House who posed varying degrees of threat, including jealous members of his own party and ambitious members in opposition. The Opposition had even gone so far as to nickname him "Robin"! Walpole's answer in dealing with such opposition was often to force such men out of power. Remove the man, remove the threat!

He was also unpopular with large sections of the community that were not powerfully represented in Parliament. These included members of the lesser gentry, the lower levels of the clergy in rural areas and the smaller craftsmen and merchants in urban centres.

But one of the biggest annoyances came from the literary hacks and great writers of the day, who were more than happy to take him to task for his policies, corruption and lifestyle. Walpole could withstand their lampooning of him, but when the attacks began to get too personal and were aimed at those he loved, he was more than ready to fight back.

Most high ranking politicians have always been the butt of the political satirist, journalist and cartoonist. The latter of this trio has always enjoyed a certain amount of freedom in lampooning his subject, while the written text, when taken too far, results in the possibility of a libel action. And so it was with Walpole. A variety of offensive and scurrilous cartoons appeared in the press, taking him to task for his corruption and policies in general. One of the most enjoyed was that of a mammoth Walpole bending over with his breeches down and displaying his huge bare buttocks while smaller sycophants were eagerly rushing to kiss his naked rump. The message of corruption in this image was more than clear.

But the writers were more abrasive in their comments. Several opposition journals were openly hostile towards him, notably 'The Craftsman', the 'London Journal', the 'Daily Post' and the 'London Evening Post'. Bolingbroke had been behind a number of damning articles in 'The Craftsman', and two radical Whigs – Thomas Gordon and John Trenchard – wrote "Cato's Letters" in the 'London Journal' in an effort to rally all honest politicians against Walpole.

Richard Francklin, the publisher of 'The Craftsman', had eight writs issued against him in four years, and even though he was fined and imprisoned in 1731, it failed to silence his journal. And opposition wasn't just confined to London. In Newcastle, a John White was prosecuted for writing and publishing alleged libellous material.

But it was the great writers who were determined to do the most damage. They were led by an indomitable quartet in the form of Henry Fielding (famous for 'Tom Jones'), Alexander Pope (noted for 'The Rape of the Lock'), John Gay ('The Beggar's Opera') and Jonathan Swift ('Gulliver's Travels'). In the third part of Swift's famous satire, set on the flying island of Laputa, hero Lemuel Gulliver finds the wise men there totally absorbed in their speculations to the exclusion of all things practical, and this is a clear and unmistakable reference to the South Sea Company.

The Irish Swift saw Walpole as the barrier to his preferment in England, and loathed him for it. He provided two character studies which amply defined his hatred for the man.

> With favour and fortune fastidiously blest,
> He's loud in his laugh and he's coarse in his jest;

Of favour and fortune unmerited vain,
A sharper in trifles, a dupe in the main.
Achieveing of nothing, still promising wonders,
By dint of experience improving in blunders;
Oppressing true merit, exalting the base,
And selling his country to purchase his peace.
A jobber of stocks by retailing false news,
A prater at court in the style of the stews,
Of virtue and worth by profession a giber,
Of juries and senates the bully and briber:
Though I name not the wretch you know who I mean -
'Tis the cur dog of Britain and spaniel of Spain.

And first: to make my observation right,
I place a statesman full before my sight,
A bloated minister in all his geer,
With shameless visage, and perfidious leer;
Two rows of teeth arm each devouring jaw;
And, ostrich-like, his all-digesting maw,
My fancy drags this monster to my view
To shew the world his chief reverse in you.
Of loud unmeaning sounds a rapid flood
Rolls from his mouth in plenteous streams of mud;
With these the court and senate-house he plies,
Made up of noise, and impudence, and lies.

In plays like 'Don Quixote' and 'Pasquin', Henry Fielding exposed the practice of bribing voters during election campaigns. Fielding's 'The Life of Mr Jonathan Wild the Great' (1743) was a savage satire on power, corruption and Walpole. Wild was a corrupt magistrate, thief taker and gang leader who was eventually caught and hanged in 1725. Fielding had no hesitation or qualms about comparing Walpole with Wild. A play entitled 'The Festival of the Golden Rump' was a vicious and unremitting attack on

Walpole. Meanwhile, in his 'Epilogue to the Satires', Pope attacked the system of 'placemen' who would happily sell their political independence and virtue to the Court.

But it would be John Gay who would cause the biggest upset and really give the literary men something to write about. In his play 'The Beggar's Opera', he portrayed Walpole as a notorious thief in the guise of Robin of Bagshot, who was also known as Gorgon, Bluff Bob and Bob Booty. The play also made clear and offensive references to Walpole's mistress, Maria Skerret. This was to prove the final straw for Walpole.

In 1737, he arranged for his friend, the Duke of Grafton, as Lord Chamberlain, to prohibit the staging of the play. All plays now had to be submitted to the Lord Chamberlain's office at least two weeks before the were due to be performed. As a result of this censorship, Gay's sequel to 'The Beggar's Opera' – 'Polly' – was prohibited.

 Such was the power of Walpole's new edict that the Lord Chamberlain's office and powers would last for a further 230 years until 1968, when the permissive dramas and pressures of the revolutionary 'Swinging Sixties' finally put an end to the quaint British anachronism of stage censorship.

And, of course, in addition to his parliamentary duties as the leader of his party and the nation, Walpole was ever mindful of his obligations to his constituents in the borough of King's Lynn. He would endeavour to return to the town whenever possible, although this was probably not as often as he would have liked or the townsfolk would have preferred. He also had his duties at Houghton to attend to as well, and this would require personal attendance, despite the sterling efforts of his steward. The other attraction of returning to his beloved Houghton was to indulge in his passion for hunting and to hold his famous Congresses. Norfolk would always play an important and defining role in shaping his character. Houghton was his bolt hole, where he could relax, unwind and enjoy a far different and quieter lifestyle from the hectic round of London gaiety and politics.

 He was a well known fellow in Lynn, and was always welcomed back by his admirers and followers when visiting the Town Hall or calling in at Henry Bell's Custom House on the Purfleet. Lynn was a big sea port, trading with the Low Countries, and, on his visits to the River Ouse waterfront, Walpole would be able to gauge the feel and mood of the ordinary man. For all his ambition, grandeur and love of power, he never really lost that essential common touch which made him popular with most people.

Returning to the town was also essential if he was to keep his supporters on side, and to ensure, in an age of bribing for votes, that he would be able to secure re-election. He was a regular patron of the town's Duke's Head Hotel where he regularly conducted business. He and his supporters always threw a grand ball at the venue on election night to celebrate his latest win and return to office.

Linnets – the quaint name given to the citizens of King's Lynn – had never been ones to stand on ceremony, especially when they had an issue to fire them up. Like Walpole, they didn't suffer fools gladly. And Walpole was no fool! There is no doubt that they would, for the most part, have been immensely proud of having the leader of the country as their own personal representative. Whatever he was to the rest of the world, he was still their 'Bob of Lynn'!

And so the country's first and longest-serving Prime Minister was free to go about his duties in the confident knowledge that his power, position and policies were virtually unassailable. His would be a long reign in office. The end would inevitably come - age, infirmity and a general lack of confidence would all help to see to that. But it was still a long way off.

7
THE DECLINE

With his domination of a successful administration, Walpole managed to achieve all his main political aims. It was inevitable, of course, that this remarkable run of political good fortune must eventually come to an end. Between 1734 and 1736, the Tory Opposition had been at a very low ebb, whereas Walpole appeared to be at the height of his political career. But, from 1737 onwards, his power started to wane as he encountered a series of personal and political setbacks.

Walpole was now in his early sixties, and his health was beginning to suffer. He had always been a stout individual, but years of entertaining combined with a healthy appetite had made him extremely corpulent. He was in constant pain from gout and kidney stones, and had, at various times, fallen ill with a variety of ailments and fevers which were partly due to overwork and nervous exhaustion. He was also prone to recurring bouts of depression and melancholy. In his final years his weight had ballooned to over 20 stone (280 lbs).

The death of Queen Caroline in November 1737 had robbed him of not only a very good friend but a willing listener and ally within the royal household. Walpole had found himself embroiled in the long-running dispute between the King and the Prince of Wales. The pair had been at loggerheads for some considerable time, and their relationship had become hateful. The Prince had moved out of the royal household and had set up his own court. He had expected, as a right, to play a leading part in political affairs. When the King had gone to Hanover, it fell to the Prince to act as Regent in his absence. Due to the Prince's arrogance and unreasonable demands, Walpole found himself at odds with the Regent and was soon out of favour. The Prince was also greatly upset by Walpole's refusal to increase his allowance.

Despite a fairly good and close personal relationship with the King, Walpole knew he always had to be careful in his dealings with the monarch. He had to allow for the King's notorious stubbornness and outbursts of temper. There had even been times when Walpole was forced to suffer the King's wrath with his unpopular decisions and George was a master at bearing grudges. As a result, Walpole found himself having to tread a very thin diplomatic line between the King and his son. With the death of the Queen, the Prime Minister found his influence and popularity at court severely curtailed.

In June 1738, Walpole was also devastated by the death of his mistress, Maria Skerret. Following the death of his first wife, he had married Maria, but she would die in childbirth just a few months later. Maria, always loyal and understanding, had provided the romantic support and sympathy which had been lacking since the breakdown of his first marriage.

Walpole's hold over the Commons was also in decline, as newer and younger M.P.s appeared on the scene. Men like William Pitt, Richard Grenville and George Lyttleton entered the House to form the core of a very effective new Opposition. They had that same passion for politics he had possessed as a young man, but now he was getting tired, often felt unwell and realised his passion for the game was nearly spent. The General Election of 1734 had guaranteed Walpole another seven years in power, but even he could see the writing on the wall when his majority in the Commons had dropped drastically to about a hundred.

Another of Walpole's ambitions, his desire to keep England out of war, was about to come crashing down around his ears, and through no fault of his own. It would be someone else's ear that would do the damage.

For almost eighteen years he had successfully kept his nation at peace. A born administrator, he had always found himself capable of his best work in peace time. But, by 1739, England's always fragile relationship with Spain had steadily worsened. English ships were in the habit of trading illegally in Spanish-controlled waters. A lucrative business had sprung up in the trading of slaves along the coasts of Spanish colonies. This had forced the Spanish to adopt an unpopular policy of boarding and searching English vessels. This practice infuriated the London merchants, whose high profits were being put in jeopardy. They turned to Walpole, insisting that he challenge what they saw as Spain's illegal right to search.

Walpole responded by negotiating the Convention of Prado, deliberately playing down the demands of the English merchants. He hoped this would maintain the peace and that the problem would eventually go away. He hadn't counted on the Opposition who demanded action, and his actions certainly didn't appease the South Sea Company either. The Company continued to press directly and independently for Spanish compensation which they considered was due to them for the boarding of their vessels. The Spanish retaliated by refusing to pay any of the compensations agreed by the Prado Convention.

So far, Walpole had managed to keep the lid on a bubbling pot of discontent, but things were about to come to a head in the form of a man called Robert Jenkins. He was the Captain of a privateer – the 'Rebecca' – and had been trading, he claimed, quite legitimately, with the Spanish territories. He had been boarded by Spanish coastguards who were in search of contraband. In the resulting fracas, Jenkins claimed that a Spaniard had produced a cutlass and severed his ear. Jenkins had wrapped the ear in cotton and placed it in a small box. On his return to England, he wasted no time in telling anyone who would listen of his terrible ordeal. Whether or not there was any truth in his story was immaterial. The production of the withered ear guaranteed Jenkins a fairly constant supply of free ale, but it also caused a great outcry of public indignation that an innocent Englishman could be treated in so harsh a fashion. The whole story was probably a complete fabrication but the public believed every word.

When pressed for details, Jenkins was credited with the reply, *"I have committed my soul to God, and my cause to my country."*

Despite Walpole's pleas for calm, the country and the Opposition went with Jenkins, demanding immediate action. The vote went against Walpole, and, in October 1739, he reluctantly declared war on Spain. The decision was immensely popular, prompting Walpole to remark, *"They now ring the bells; they will soon wring their hands."* But the War of Jenkins's Ear (1739-41), as it become known, was a conflict which would merge into the more damaging War of Austrian Succession (1740-48). With Europe now in turmoil once more, the impending crisis had led Walpole, in a speech to the Commons on 13th February 1741, to make his famous reference to "The Balance of Power".

When a number of European countries disputed the succession of Maria Theresa following the death of her father, the Emperor Charles VI, in 1740, Austria, supported by England and Holland, was forced to go to war against the combined forces of Prussia, France and Spain. All of Walpole's efforts to preserve peace had been overcome by the Opposition, press and public.

Walpole was now fighting a steadily losing battle in Parliament, struggling to survive for another two and a half years. His conduct of a war he never wanted and didn't believe in caused much criticism. Various factions joined the Opposition against him, as he lost the confidence of the House and the loyalty of his colleagues. It was only the King's support that kept him in office plus the dilemma of who should replace him if he was to go. Another problem facing his opponents was just how to get rid of such a powerful figure. He managed to survive a censure motion against him and prepared to fight yet another General Election in 1741. It was a keenly contested campaign, which, in theory, Walpole won, but his majority in the House had been cut to a mere nineteen, making him highly vulnerable to Opposition attacks against him.

Faced with several by-election defeats, he managed to survive a committee of inquiry into the conduct of the war by just three votes. In a packed House, he had polled 253 votes to 250. The Great Man knew it was time to go, and, on 11th February 1742, he reluctantly resigned all his posts. The King, reduced to tears at his leaving, had begged him to stay, but to no avail.

But he was still a force to be reckoned with, and, two days before his resignation, he accepted a peerage to the Lords, where he acted as an adviser, supporter and confidant to his Whig friends who were still in power. He had accepted the Earldom of Orford, reviving a now dormant title, in honour of his old friend, Edward Russell, Earl of Orford.

At this time, one of his old enemies, William Pulteney, had been created Earl of Bath. Walpole remarked to the new Earl, *"My Lord Bath, you and I are now as insignificant men as any in England."*

With his health now steadily deteriorating, he returned to Houghton to rest. He had tried many remedies throughout his life, the most unusual being to take one ounce of Alicante soap in three pints of lime water a day. By the time he died it was estimated that he had consumed about 180 pounds of soap and swallowed 1,200 gallons of lime water.

He found retirement dull. He tried to find solace in his splendid library, but, according to the memoirs of Mrs Piozzi, '...when pulling down a book and holding it some minutes to his eyes, he suddenly and seemingly sullenly exchanged it for another. He held that about half as long, and looking out a third returned it instantly to its shelf and burst into tears. *"I have led a life of business so long,"* said he, *"that I have lost my taste for reading, and now – what shall I do?"*

Too frail to pursue his passions of hunting and riding, he would travel his vast estate in his carriage, surveying the land he had planted as his monument. In a letter, dated 24th June 1743, he wrote, *" This place affords no news, no subject of amusement and entertainment to you fine Gentlemen. Men of wit and pleasure about town understand not the language, nor taste the charms of the inanimate world; my flatterers here are all mutes, the Oaks, the Beeches and the Chestnuts seem to contend, which shall best please the Lord of the Mannor: They cannot deceive, they will not lie."*

In the Autumn of 1744 he left his beloved Houghton for the last time and returned to London. By now he was in great pain from the kidney stones and internal haemorrhages which had been plaguing him for several months. In their efforts to relieve his suffering, his doctors did more harm than good. It was only his strong constitution and will which helped him to stay alive, plus the large doses of opium administered to deaden the pain. A vile healing remedy known as the Lixivium Lithontripticum provided such a violent reaction that it did considerable damage to his poor body. There was even a suggestion that one of his doctors was a Catholic sympathiser who administered poison by way of revenge for Walpole's treatment of the Catholics. There is, however, absolutely no evidence to prove this one way or the other.

As he lay on his death bed at his home in Arlington Street, his son Horace took down his last words:-

"Dear Horace this Lixivium has blown me up. It has tore me to peices. The Affair is over with me....Give me more opium; knock me down. I expect nothing but to have ease. Dear Horace if one must die, 'tis hard to die in pain. Why do you all stand round me! are ye all waiting there, because this is the last night...'Tis impossible not to be a little disturb'd at going out of the world, but you see I am not afraid."

Robert Walpole died on 18th March 1745. The autopsy on his body was performed by Sir Caesar

Hawkins. Walpole had so many bladder stones that Horace believed his father had been killed by a 'lithotriptic' medicine. The body was returned to Houghton and buried in the family vault of St Martin's.

No monument was erected to his memory. An entry was made in the parish register :- 'A.D. 1745, the Right Hon. Robert, Earl of Orford, died March 18th, and was buried ye 25th, in ye 68th year of his age.

Exactly five months after his death, that which Sir Robert had always dreaded - and had spent all his political life fighting against – came to pass. On 19th August 1745, the young Prince Charles Edward Stuart, "Bonnie Prince Charlie", raised his standard at Glenfinnan, proclaimed his father James VIII of Scotland and James III of England, and himself as Regent. Rallying the Scottish clans to his cause, he marched south into England. His route took him through Carlisle, Penrith, Kendal, Lancaster, Preston, Manchester, Macclesfield and Leek before arriving at Derby. The City of London was thrown into a state of panic. The invading army was a mere 127 miles from the capital. Then the decision was made to retreat. With George II's forces, under the brutal Duke of Cumberland, in pursuit, the Scots were finally beaten on 16th April 1746 at the Battle of Culloden. It was the last great battle to be fought on British soil and ended the hopes of the Stuart dynasty ever regaining the throne.

The Great Man, who must have been turning in his grave, could now rest in peace!

8
CATHERINE AND MARIA

Robert Walpole was one month away from his twenty-fourth birthday when he married Catherine Shorter, an attractive girl in her eighteenth year. Equally attractive for the Colonel was the handsome dowry she brought with her, which helped her new father-in-law to pay off some of his outstanding debts and mortgages. Hers was a passionate nature, and she and her new husband seemed well suited as they settled down to married life at the old manor hall at Houghton. Being a teenager and eager to please her spouse, she displayed no signs of the temperament, jealousy and lack of self-control which would eventually blight the relationship. Walpole loved her and did his best to please his bride.

At the time of her marriage, there were no signs of Walpole becoming the great and influential figure of future years. He hadn't even entered Parliament at this point. It had been yet another example of the fairly traditional custom of families of note and wealth within the East Anglian area joining forces by marriage. Catherine probably felt a little put out when her sister, Charlotte, married Francis Seymour, 1st Baron Conway. Their son, also Francis, would eventually become the 1st Marquess of Hartford.

In 1701, Catherine proudly presented her husband with a son and heir. The boy was named Robert after his father and grandfather. Over the next five years she gave birth to three more children – Catherine (1703), Mary (1704) and Edward (1706). Up to this point, and with such a regular production of offspring, things certainly appeared to be quite happy within the Walpole household. But gradually – influenced in her upbringing by her grandmother, Lady Phillips – Catherine's true nature began to emerge. She had been groomed for society, and was not content with her role as a country wife.

Around the time of young Edward's birth in 1706, Catherine had quarrelled violently with Walpole's beloved sister, Dorothy. The latter, always known to the family as Dolly, must have been so upset by the confrontation that she fled from Houghton, taking refuge with Lady Wharton. But when the rakish Lord Wharton had caught Dolly's eye, Walpole promptly stepped in and ordered his sister to leave the Wharton household. Dolly then retired to Norfolk in the company of the Townshends. Townshend had fallen for Dolly's charms and, when his wife died, he wasted no time in marrying his best friend's sister.

With Dolly safely installed at Raynham, Catherine was now the undisputed mistress of Houghton at last. But, after such a passionate start to the marriage, the atmosphere between her and her husband had become increasingly unhappy. Catherine's violent rages and her jealous streak played a significant part in the marital disharmony. Walpole was now well embarked on his new and successful political career and found it increasingly difficult to devote all the time and attention to his wife that she craved.

Despite the gradual breakdown of the marriage, Walpole and Catherine came to a mutual agreement to stay together for the sake of their young family and also for appearances. And so they decided to lead private lives, endeavouring to be as discreet as possible. They would, however, still be seen together whenever protocol and circumstances required.

Having been raised in London by her grandmother, Catherine had grown to hate Houghton life with its boring rural routine. She much preferred the wild life of London, bringing with it the social whirl of society balls and soirées, visits to the opera and the theatre and the gaiety of the Vauxhall Gardens. The public garden at Vauxhall, established in 1661, was a fashionable meeting place and a site of lavish entertainments for almost two hundred years until its closure in 1859.

Catherine, enjoying her new found freedom, embarked on a series of affairs. Walpole, well aware of his wife's indiscretions, had no qualms about them, having taken to brief dalliances with a number of mistresses whenever he felt the need. These amours on his part were usually short-lived and quickly forgotten.

On his first arrival in London to take up his new parliamentary duties as an M.P., Walpole had lived with Lady Phillips at her home in Berkeley Street. By 1705, however, he and his wife had moved to a house on the east side of Dover Street, off Piccadilly and just a short walk from Lady Phillips's residence. In 1715, still maintaining a fairly unified marital front, the couple moved to a new house at nearby 17, Arlington Street in the St. James's district, which Walpole would also use as his political headquarters.

Two years later, in September 1717, Catherine presented Walpole with their fifth child, Horace. By now, London society was well aware of the couple's marital rift and the separate lives they led. It didn't take long for rumours to circulate to the effect that the new arrival was not the true son of Robert Walpole. Various names were bandied about, but the general consensus of opinion was that Carr Hervey, the older brother of Lord John Hervey, was, in fact, the father. This suggestion would persist for some considerable time, especially when it became clear that the young Horace bore no notable resemblance to his sibling brothers or his father, either in looks or demeanour.

Walpole, however, whatever his personal thoughts on the matter, immediately accepted the boy as his son without question. And, as he grew up, Horace would always look upon Walpole as his true father, eventually coming to inherit the property of Houghton in his seventies.

And so Walpole and Catherine continued to live out their sham of a marriage until her death on 20th August 1737, in her fifty fifth year.

After a series of casual affairs, Walpole had eventually met a woman he really loved. His latest and last mistress was a vivacious Irish lady called Maria Skerret.* She was the only daughter of Thomas Skerret, a wealthy London merchant. Walpole was smitten by her beauty, intelligence and loyalty, and she amazed those who knew her by responding to her older lover with surprising devotion. In 1725, Maria gave birth to Walpole's illegitimate daughter, who was also called Maria**

Maria Skerret indulged in the popular passion for shell work. She made a grotto of shells, which caused the Duchess of Portland to scathingly remark, *"It is a 'shellery', for 'grotto' I will not call it."* Apparently, the Duchess had found the regularity of Maria's shells *"abominable"* and that she had gone so far as to paint her coral red!

In 1735, Walpole was worried about Maria's condition when she became desperately ill "of a pleuritic fever". Maria's plight had reached the ears of Queen Caroline who, in conversation with Lord Hervey, asked many questions about Miss Skerret. She enquired about the lady's beauty and understanding, and Walpole's obvious fondness and weakness for her. The Queen was glad he had an amusement for his leisure hours, but could not understand how a man of Walpole's age (he was 59), with *"...his dirty mouth and great belly"*, could induce any woman to love him except for his money.

That the relationship should last so long speaks volumes about the genuine love Walpole and Maria felt for each other. Following Catherine's death, Walpole, after a suitable if brief period of respectful mourning, wasted no time in marrying the now pregnant Maria in 1738. She, for her part, brought a handsome dowry of £30,000 to the marriage, of which her husband was suitably appreciative! The couple now looked forward to a happy life together in Walpole's later years.

But tragedy was to strike when, within a few brief months, Maria was to die in childbirth in June 1738. The baby she carried, a girl, was stillborn. The dead infant was named Catherine, in memory of Walpole's beloved elder daughter, who had died in 1722. Maria and her child were duly buried in the family crypt beneath the altar of St. Martin's Church at Houghton, alongside the coffin of the recently deceased Catherine Shorter. Walpole was devastated at the loss of his beautiful Maria. For the remaining few years of his life, he would put all thoughts of other women behind him.

---

*   *Various sources also give the spelling as Skerrett and Skerritt.*
**   *Also referred to as Mary in some sources.*

9
BROTHERS AND SISTERS

Discounting the likely possibility of any illegitimate offspring resulting from Sir Robert's various liaisons with his other mistresses,* the official tally of children to bear the Walpole name was seven. Five were born to Catherine,** and the remaining two to Maria.

Robert Walpole achieved an heir with his firstborn son, Robert, born in 1701. Like his father, he was educated at Eton. By the age of 22, in 1723, the young man was created a peer, taking the title Lord Walpole of Walpole. For most of 1722-23 he spent much of the period abroad on his Grand Tour, and was the first of the Walpole brothers to visit Europe with the intention of bringing back various works of art for his father's growing collection

He would marry the 16-year-old Margaret Rolle, daughter of Samuel Rolle of Heanton Satchville in Devon. She brought with her a substantial dowry in rents and money, plus the control of the boroughs of Callington and Ashburton, and the reversion of the Barony of Clinton. She would later become Baroness Clinton.

From the start of the marriage, it was clear that young Robert and his teenage bride had no real affection for each other. The couple lived in London and Norfolk, their Norfolk home being Crostwight Hall, lying between the town of North Walsham and the coast. In 1730, when Robert was in his late twenties, his wife presented him with their only child, a son called George.

The marriage having irretrievably broken down, both Robert and Margaret continued to be both mutually and persistently unfaithful. It was rumoured that the M.P. Sir George Oxenden was the real father of the newly born George. Lord Hervey, in his diary, wrote that Oxenden *"...had debauched the wife of the eldest son of his friend, benefactor and patron, Sir Robert Walpole"*.

In 1734, Margaret eloped with her latest lover, Thomas Sturgess, a fellow of King's, and promptly went abroad with him. In 1745, Robert would inherit his father's estate, and with it the title of 2nd Earl of Orford. Less welcome would be a debt of some £40,000 to £50,000, incurred by his father through the lavish building of the new Houghton Hall.

In his biography of Horace Walpole, Norfolk historian R.W. Ketton-Cremer tells how Horace once came across an illegitimate half-sister who had fallen on hard times. He had been able to help her by giving her accommodation at Strawberry Hill.
**Ketton-Cremer also wrote that Robert and Catherine had a son called William, who died young, but no other source confirms this.*

Within a further six years, in 1751, Robert would also be dead, the title and the Hall passing to his son, George. The latter, without doubt, was to prove to be one of the most fascinating and intriguing of the Walpoles after his illustrious grandfather and famous Uncle Horace. The undisputed black sheep of the Walpole family, George justly deserves a chapter to himself.

In 1703, Catherine Shorter had given birth to her second child, a daughter, Catherine***, and a sister for the young Robert. The child would become the apple of her devoted father's eye, but her short life was to be blighted by almost continual illness.

It was in the autumn of 1720 that Walpole, already immersed in the complexities of the South Sea Company scandal, became increasingly concerned about his daughter's latest bout of illness. She was prone to violent fits, fainting and prolonged bouts of sickness and was being treated by the family doctor, Sir Hans Sloane. He decided to send her to Bath, in the company of her governess, Mrs Bedford, to be put in the care of a Dr Cheyne, who prescribed her taking the waters at Bristol. But her condition worsened and she was rushed back to Bath. Eventually she seemed to rally, giving Walpole hope of a recovery. Dr Cheyne kept Walpole regularly appraised of Catherine's condition in the letters he sent from Bath to Walpole's home at Chelsea.

The girl's condition was deteriorating rapidly and she was in almost constant pain. In this distressing condition, she continued to exist until 11th October 1722, when she died of consumption. Her passing was a tremendous blow for her father.

In 1704, a year after Catherine's birth, another daughter, Mary, arrived on the scene. She would go on to marry George, Viscount Malpas, the son and heir of George, Earl of Cholmondeley in Cheshire. Their union would eventually change the destiny of Houghton when, in 1797, their grandson, George James, 4th Earl and 1st Marquess of Cholmondeley, would become the new owner of Houghton Hall. Mary, however, would not live to see it, dying young at the age of 28 in 1732, and leaving her father another daughter to grieve over.

The birth of Walpole's fourth child and second son, Edward, in 1706, was to eventually provide the basis for one of Houghton's most charming love stories. He was a handsome, impetuous, generous and passionate young man, who was renowned for his witty conversation. He became the M.P. for Lostwithiel, and later for Yarmouth, received a Knighthood and was eventually appointed to the post of Chief Secretary of Ireland. A lover of the arts, he was a gifted musician and played the bass-viol to great acclaim at private concerts given by Frederick, Prince of Wales. There were times, however, when the talented Edward would be

*** Some sources quote Katherine

at odds with his younger brother, Horace, due mainly to Edward's jealousy of his brother's social, political and intellectual successes.

Like his brothers, Edward had also done the obligatory Grand Tour. In Italy, in 1730, he had become so ill with a raging fever that he had not been expected to recover.

At the age of 28 he met and fell in love with a beauty called Dorothy Clement. The daughter of Hammond Clement and his wife, Priscilla, she was born about 1715. Her father was the post-master at Darlington. Dorothy had been working as a seamstress in a second-hand clothes shop in London's Pall Mall, just opposite the recently completed Marlborough House. Edward courted his new love but any hope of marriage was promptly dashed when his father adamantly refused to such a union, in view of Dorothy's lack of social status.

Nevertheless, the couple remained devoted to each other until Dorothy's early death in about 1739, when she was approximately 24-years-old. She bore him five children. Four of these would grow to adulthood – Laura, Maria, Edward and Charlotte. Of this quartet, it was to be Maria, a striking beauty, who would create the greatest sensation.

Maria married James, 2nd Earl Waldegrave, presenting him with three charming daughters – Elizabeth Laura, Charlotte Maria and Horatia. Laura went on to marry George, 4th Lord Waldegrave, Charlotte wed Lord Euston and Horatia became the wife of Captain Hugh Conway Seymour, R.N.

This delightful trio were known collectively in society circles as The Ladies Waldegrave. As girls, they would have their portrait painted by a talented artist , George James, and this painting is one of the most admired by visitors to Houghton today. In later life, as young women, they were again painted, this time by none other than Sir Joshua Reynolds. This portrait is now part of the National Gallery of Scotland's collection in Edinburgh. Both James and Reynolds titled their portraits 'The Ladies Waldegrave'.

With the eventual death of the Earl Waldegrave, Maria would then go on to make a second successful marriage to William Henry, Duke of Gloucester, brother of the future King George III. In view of her background, her entry into royal circles would prove to be a frequently hostile affair, but she managed to weather the impending storms within the Royal Family remarkably well.

Considering that she had been the illegitimate daughter of a seamstress, there can be no doubt that, in marrying both an earl and a duke, she had done very well for herself indeed!

Edward died in 1784, well into his mid-seventies. Unlike his two brothers, he would never become the master of Houghton.

On 24th September 1717, ten years since the birth of her fourth child, Catherine provided Robert

Pictured left: 17 Arlington Street, Robert Walpole's London residence. Author's Collection.
Right: Stone Hall. © Houghton Hall.

King's Lynn map, 1725. Sir Robert Walpole. Author's Collection.

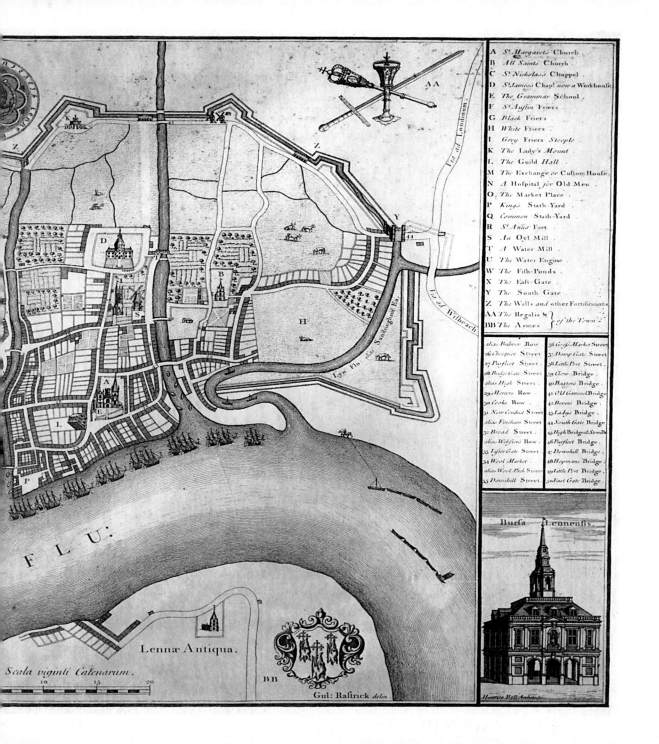

Pictured top: Stables, Houghton - viewed from the South East. Author's Collection.
Bottom: Stables and white deer. © Houghton Hall.

Walpole with another son, Horace. The society gossips were eager to spread the rumour that Carr Hervey was the father and not Walpole. Because of the breakdown in the marriage, it seems almost certain that Walpole was not responsible, but as to whether or not paternity should be laid at Carr Hervey's door is a matter of pure speculation. Walpole accepted the child without hesitation, thus giving Horace the eventual birthright to Houghton, albeit not until he was well into his seventies.

A studious and fastidious child, Horace proved to be the true scholar of the family. A Whig M.P. for Castle Rising and King's Lynn from 1741-67, he became one of the most outstanding literary figures of his day. In 1764, he wrote the first Gothic novel, "The Castle of Otranto", a tale of supernatural terror in Italy, and more than 4,000 of his letters would be published. As an ardent observer of society, his diaries and letters give a remarkable insight into the events and characters of the 18th century.

He left Houghton at the earliest opportunity and very rarely returned. He did, however, pay the briefest of visits to the estate in 1761. On 25th March he wrote to George Montagu :- *"Here I am at Houghton! And alone! in this spot where (except for two hours last month) I have not been in sixteen years!... Here I am, probably for the last time of my life, though not for the last time; every clock that strikes tells me I am an hour nearer to yonder church – that church into which I have not yet had courage to enter, where lies that mother on whom I doated, and who doated on me!... There, too, lies he who founded its greatness, to contribute to whose fall Europe was embroiled."*

Horace was only 43-years-old when he wrote this letter, and, probably mindful that life expectancy would only grant him a possible further decade, could have no idea he would live well into his late seventies!

He moved to Strawberry Hill, his Gothic mansion in Twickenham, then a separate town southwest of London. He had purchased the house and estate of five acres in 1749 for £776-10s-0d . The Saracen's Head was present throughout the house, just as at Houghton, and was intended to remind one of Walpole's ancestral connections with the Crusades.

Horace was always a frail man who suffered from gout. At dinner he would eat moderately of chicken, pheasant or any light food. He disliked pastry and drank iced water.

Writing about Horace, Thomas Macaulay would describe him as *"...the most eccentric, the most artificial, the most fastidious and the most capricious of men."*

In 1791, at the age of 74, Horace would finally inherit his father's house at Houghton on the death of his nephew, George. In doing so, Horace also became 4th Earl of Orford. Although he had never really liked or appreciated the grand Hall, he was appalled to find Houghton in a terrible state, a result of George's neglect. The great external staircases were gone, the fine collection of paintings were sold and water was coming down the interior walls due to the lack of repairs. Seeing the damage, and in reference to his father, Horace wrote, *"For what has he built Houghton? For his grandson to annihilate, and his son to mourn over!"* In the short time left to him, Horace would do what he could to repair some of the damage done to the house.

On 2nd March 1797, at the age of 79, Horace died. Houghton now passed through the female line to the Cholmondeley family. He had left his beloved Strawberry Hill to his niece, the sculptress Anne Seymour Damer, for her lifetime. In 1810, she found the house too expensive to keep, so she relinquished the ownership to the eventual heir, Lady Elizabeth Laura Waldegrave, the granddaughter of Sir Edward Walpole.

The contents of Strawberry Hill were sold in 1842, the proceeds of the sale totalling £33,450-11s-9d. The house was later sold to the De Stern family who owned it from 1883 to 1923, when it was sold to St. Mary's College, as a girls' school.

One might have expected Horace to be laid to rest close to his beloved Strawberry Hill at Twickenham. But, as he had already hinted in his letter to George Montagu thirty six years earlier, his body was interred in the family vault at Houghton. In death he was reunited with the man he had always considered to be his true father.

An entry in the parish register simply read :-
"Horace Walpole, late Earl of Orford, aged 80 years, was buried
Martch ye 13th, 1797. A bachelor."

Maria's illegitimate daughter Maria, born in 1725, became legitimised in 1738 on the marriage of her mother to Robert Walpole. She was thus able, in due course, to make a successful and acceptable marriage to Colonel Charles Churchill of Chalfont.

A few months later, Catherine, her only sibling by Maria Skerret, was stillborn.

10
HOUGHTON HALL

The old manor house at Houghton had been mainly built by Walpole's grandfather, Edward, in the reign of Charles II, although there were traces within it of building styles ranging from the 15th to the 17th centuries. By 1720, Robert Walpole had extended the estate to some 9,400 acres.

Having reached the pinnacle of his career, Robert Walpole realised he needed a new house that would reflect his newly acquired power and position. His decision to build a new hall at Houghton was, however, pre-empted by a letter he received in 1721 from his steward, James Rolfe, at the old manor house. In a state of some agitation, Rolfe had written to his master that, *"...I have a thousand ungrateful Companions the Mice...they run in such great numbers 'tis impossible to think of destroying them unless the whole house be removed."* It seems the vermin were nibbling away at Sir Robert's documents, and the whole house would indeed need to be removed.

And so a decision was made to commence work on a new hall, a task that would take a total of thirteen years to complete. But, in that relatively short space of time, Walpole removed not only the old hall, but also the stable block and the old village of Houghton, replacing them with a fine mansion, magnificent stables and a new village.

The original designer of the house was to be a young and promising architect called James Gibbs. It seems that Walpole then had a change of heart and hired the better known and well established Sir Colen Campbell. Campbell, a Scotsman, had originally trained as a lawyer before becoming an architect. A great admirer of the great Italian Renaissance architect Andrea Palladio (1518-1580), he built houses of an 'Italianate' classicism distilled from a mixture of Palladio and Inigo Jones. His better known houses would include Wanstead, Essex (1715 – demolished 1824); Ebberston, Yorkshire (1718); Mereworth, Tonbridge, Kent; and Stourhead, Stourton, Wilts (1721). His greatest achievement would be the new hall at Houghton.

Campbell's design impressed Walpole, providing the latter with a solid, rectangular domicile, flanked by two square dependencies which were linked to the main house by two short, curving, enclosed colonnades. Access to the 'piano nobile' would be by two majestic stone staircases. Entrance to the house would be from the East Front. The dependency to the south would mainly house the kitchens and storage areas, the one to north was intended for an orangery, chapel and laundry court. Looking at the building today, the straight lines and sweeping curves of Palladian balance are clearly in evidence, but the sight of four stone domes on the corners of the main house occasionally provoke interest and curiosity. It is felt that the designs of Gibbs and

Stone Hall. © Houghton Hall.

Common Parlour, Houghton. © Houghton Hall.

Campbell overlapped to some extent, with Walpole seeing the obvious merits in both. It has been assumed that the domes are pure Gibbs, with the rest of the dwelling being attributed to Campbell. The view of the domes from a distance gives the Hall an added grandeur.

The interiors of the Hall were entrusted to William Kent (1686-1748), a much admired painter, architect, furniture designer, interior decorator and landscape gardener. A jovial, extrovert and good-humoured Yorkshireman of humble origins, he had begun his career as a coach painter before being sent to Rome by a consortium of wealthy patrons to study art. In the world of architecture, he was foremost in introducing the Palladian style into England from Italy. He believed that each room of a house should be a separate and individual work of art. It was also his belief that furniture was an essential part of proper interior decoration. Later, he would be at the forefront of the 18th century Gothic revival and in Romantic landscape gardening. Horace Walpole considered him to be "the father of modern gardening". However, according to Horace, Sir Robert had a low opinion of Kent's powers as a colourist, and this view accounts for the muted and paler colours on the ceilings at Houghton, which had been toned down from Kent's brighter hues at Walpole's insistence.

Horace also said of Kent's portraits that they *"...bore little resemblance to the persons that sat for them; and the colouring was worse, more raw and undetermined than that of the most errant journey man to the profession"*. This remark by Horace may have helped to give rise to the totally unfounded speculation that Kent may have suffered from some form of colour blindness.

Kent's work speaks for itself in his decoration of Chiswick House, Holkham Hall and Kensington Palace. At Houghton his task was great and his contribution to the interior design immense, being responsible for all the painted ceilings, most of the original furniture and the Italian marble fireplaces. The painted canvas which lines the walls of the Grand Staircase is believed to have been painted by Kent himself, and it is also presumed that his was the architectural design for the spacious new stable block to the south of the Hall.

In addition to his own team of craftsmen, artisans and labourers, Kent would bring in the talents of two other notable masters. All the stucco and plaster work was assigned to the renowned Italian stuccoist, Giuseppe Artari, who came from Venice and often worked with his brother. The sculpture work was given to John Michael Rysbrack. Rysbrack (1694-1770) was a meticulous sculptor who was born in Antwerp. Settling in England in 1720, he became famous for his busts, his tombs in Westminster Abbey, and the equestrian statue of William III, erected in Queen Square, Bristol in 1735. Two of the finest examples of his work – a fine Roman-style bust of Walpole and a superbly carved overmantle, 'The Sacrifice to Bacchus'- can be seen at Houghton. Both he and Artari would also employ their own teams of craftsmen on the site.

The actual task of building Houghton was given to Thomas Ripley, a former carpenter who was senior officer of the Board of Works. A fine builder, his later talents as an architect would be employed by Sir Robert's brother, Horatio, in the building of Wolterton Hall, near Aylsham in the heart of Norfolk.

Work began in earnest on 24th May 1722 with the laying of the foundation stone on the south-east corner. The workforce employed on the overall project must have been tremendous, with labourers demolishing old buildings and erecting their replacements. As soon as each new section had been constructed, the craftsmen moved in to add the fine detail and design of the interiors. The site teemed with a variety of rich and varied raw materials, most of which had to be transported to the port of King's Lynn before onward transmission to Houghton in horse and ox drawn wagons, a distance of some fifteen miles over rough roads and rutted tracks.

The wagons contained Honduran mahogany, Yorkshire and Devonshire stone, and marbles from Italy and Plymouth. Closer to home, they also hauled local Snettisham carrstone for the stable block and vast quantities of Norfolk red brick.

With its grand staircase, benches, doors and door cases, Houghton is believed to contain the most mahogany of any house in Britain. A scurrilous rumour persisted that Walpole had deliberately removed the heavy duty on rare woods during the period it took to fill the house with mahogany, and that he then proceeded not only to replace the tax but to double it! By the time Walpole came to build Houghton, the duty on timber had already been removed under the Naval Stores Act of 1721, following the intense lobbying of angry timber merchants. The removal of the tax took effect from June 1722, shortly after work on the Hall had begun, and it wasn't reimposed until well into 1724.

Thomas Ripley already knew the value of working in mahogany, having used it to good effect on a large scale at the Admiralty Office in 1723. It was a rich, dark, durable wood that didn't splinter and was impervious to worm. Ripley recommended the use of mahogany in preference to oak and deal, ordering his requirements in mid-1724. The entire shipment amounted to just under 30,000 feet, or about 60 tons. The cost was about four pence to five pence a foot. At approximately £600 overall, this represented a very reasonable outlay for Walpole. The timber was shipped to London in three loads - 305 planks carried on the 'Loyal Betty', 88 planks on the 'Rose' and 26 planks aboard the 'Dolphin'. Of the original 419 planks, only 391 were recorded as being off-loaded at King's Lynn. The rest, it seems, was used to construct a mahogany staircase in a house in Spitalfields for a Mr Marmaduke Smith. A Yorkshire-born carpenter and builder, he was a close associate of Thomas Ripley.

Thanks to Ripley's decision to use mahogany, Walpole never had to suffer the embarrassment of some members of the landed gentry who were sold fake 'mahogany' by rogue builders, in the belief that they were purchasing the genuine article. It had been the practice of dishonest carpenters to pass off oak richly stained with bulls' blood. By the time the bill had been paid and the oak was beginning to split, the deceivers were long gone.

For the marble needed for all the fireplaces and the decoration of the Marble Parlour dining room, Ripley opted for mainly Italian Carrara marbles with their rich colours, hewn from quarries near Carrara in the Apuan Alps. Considered to be the purest and most expensive of marbles, it was used by the Romans and by Michelangelo. But for the pink columns in the Parlour he chose the subtle shades of a Plymouth marble known as 'Fleur de Peche' (or peach flower).

The outside of the Hall was to be faced with a hard wearing and beautiful Jurassic sandstone, quarried at Aislaby near Whitby, in North Yorkshire. This stone was transported down the North Sea to The Wash by barges and ships which would discharge their heavy cargoes at Lynn. Meanwhile, the imposing white stone of the Stone Hall was being hewn from a quarry at Beer on the Devon coast, before beginning its long journey through the Channel and up to Norfolk. The logistics of moving so much heavy and valuable raw material were quite remarkable.

Meanwhile, thousands of locally produced red bricks were being carried to the site to form the inner core of the house and the vaulting for the stables, and tons of soft, light brown sandstone, known as carrstone, were being dug out of the Snettisham site just a few miles from the new Hall.

By 1725, the main shell had been erected. In that year, the first of several gilded, pennant-shaped weathervanes appeared on Gibbs's south-west dome. The last vane would be put in place in 1729. In more recent years, these vanes have all been splendidly re-gilded, restoring them to their former glory.

As the house took shape, evidence of Walpole's allegorical and symbolic references soon became apparent. Visitors would enter by a huge door at the top of the stone steps on the East Front. Above their heads were Rysbrack's external figures of Neptune and Britannia, a clear allusion to Walpole as the guardian of the nation and the ruler of the seas. On the West Front, massive Ionic columns rose up from the steps to a grand pediment, into which was carved the families' coats of arms. On a plinth at the peak of the pediment stood a fine statue of Demosthenes, defender of liberty, flanked, on his right by Justice, with her sword and scales, and, on his left, by Minerva, the Goddess of Wisdom. The message was clear to all. This was the house of a wise, just and fair politician. The presence of Demosthenes also indicated that Walpole, like the noble Greek, was a fine orator.

Construction at Houghton was not without its mishaps. In addition to the normal and expected

Saloon, Houghton. © *Houghton Hall.*

Marble Parlour, Houghton. © Houghton Hall.

accidents on such a huge development, the builders suffered a temporary but annoying setback due to a fire in 1732.

The Hall would consist of 106 rooms and outhouses, and it would be a proud boast that it was possible to make up 110 beds at an hour's notice. As each part of the building took shape, the craftsmen moved in to work on the interiors. Kent, Rysbrack and Artari moved between Houghton and other commissions while they waited for each new part of the house to be made ready for their attention. Kent spent a great deal of his time moving back and forth between Houghton and nearby Holkham, which was also under construction.

By 1735, with Walpole in his 58th year and a mere ten years away from his eventual demise, the Hall was finally completed. During its construction, of course, parts of it had already been occupied and used as they became ready for purpose. The chapel was the only part of the property unfinished at the time of Walpole's death. Walpole had little need for a chapel with St. Martin's Church just a short walk away across the Park.

The cavernous interior of the Stone Hall was a 40-foot cube, and based on the one designed by Inigo Jones for the Queen's House at Greenwich. With this and the vast rooms and high ceilings of the other state rooms on the 'piano nobile', Kent and his team were faced with a daunting challenge. It was a Sistine Chapel scenario on a slightly smaller scale, requiring a network of wooden scaffolding, planking and step ladders. A series of richly decorated paintings with classical themes would decorate the ceilings on the north side in a deliberate attempt to impress Sir Robert's guests.

A decision on Walpole's part to replace a planned three-roomed state apartment with a dining room and a Cabinet on the north-east corner presented Kent with the chance to design his most outstanding ceiling of the whole complex. A ceiling and fireplace festooned with painted, gilded, plastered and carved grapes was not only a tribute to Bacchus but also to Walpole's love of good wines. He had a particular penchant for Château Margaux and Château Lafite.

Other ceilings featured Flora, the Goddess of Flowers, Aurora, Goddess of the Dawn, and Venus. The latter was not only considered to be the Goddess of Love, but was versatile enough for the early Georgians to be regarded as the goddess for sleep and country living as well. The second state bedroom, now squeezed into an originally planned dressing room, sported a painting of the handsome shepherd boy, Endymion, being put into a deep sleep by his admirer Selene (or Luna), the Moon Goddess, in an attempt to preserve his incredible beauty. The lofty heights of The Saloon displayed a magnificently painted mosaic surrounding an octagon in which Apollo is seen driving his chariot of the Sun.

The most intriguing ceiling was that of the Cabinet, with Minerva, Goddess of Wisdom, holding a shield bearing the Walpole coat of arms and treading on the hideous creature of Envy. This was Walpole's own personal joke, it being his intention that everyone should be envious of his new home. The most envious would be his own brother-in-law, 'Turnip' Townshend, who realised Walpole's new hall was a far grander affair than his own smaller mansion at nearby Raynham. The joke, however, would soon backfire on Walpole when the equally impressive Holkham Hall, home of the Cokes of Norfolk, reached completion.

Things were much easier for Kent on the south side, this being the Walpole family's private apartments. The ceilings were plain, the gilding on the woodwork and doors non-existent. Always anxious to save money, Walpole saw no need to decorate quarters that only relatives, close friends and servants would see. His only concession was the beautifully created emblem of the Order of the Garter displayed prominently on the ceiling of the Yellow Drawing Room.

The use of mahogany was greatly in evidence throughout the 'piano nobile', being used for the decorative benches in the Stone Hall, the balustrade of the Great Staircase, and all the doors. The doors are amazing creations of solid mahogany, each weighing some 3-4 hundredweight (336-448 lbs), and operating on rising butts. Most of the brass hinges have no screws to hold them in place, the brackets being fixed by tightly fitting wedges. The larger, bottom two central panels of each door display a vertical grain, whereas the smaller upper panel has the grain moving in a horizontal direction. This was a clever device employed by master carpenters to create a symmetry and to stop the eye being taken off the top of the door.

The doors at Houghton also played a vital role in preserving that essential Palladian balance. It is not immediately obvious at first glance, but several doors on the 'piano nobile' are false, all there to create an image of symmetrical design. A three-sided balcony on the second-floor level of the Stone Hall has a total of nine doors, five of which are false. A further two false doors are located in the Marble Parlour, another in the Cabinet. All are made of the same solid mahogany as the originals, and all have key holes and handles. The only giveaway is the lack of hinges.

Another use of the mahogany came with the construction of Walpole's study and library, with massive bookcases providing an imposing home for the many fine tomes which filled their shelves. The room still houses Walpole's desk, chair and day bed.

Houghton also boasted its fair share of false windows as well, as can be seen from the large fake frames of the first state bedroom and the Cabinet, as well as the bricked up areas of the northern wall of the south dependency. Knowing Walpole's desire to save money at any opportunity, this could be seen as an attempt to avoid the Window Tax which had first been imposed in 1691. The truth, however, was yet another attempt to preserve the vital balance.

The new house would also provide a number of hidden delights and obvious curiosities. The most unusual was the arrangement of the Marble Parlour, one floor up and some considerable distance from the kitchen area. This was a deliberate ploy to avoid the risk of fire, not to mention unpleasant smells, and the noise of cooking and servants. This meant that hot food, walked through the lower part of the house and up a staircase, would be cooling down by the time it reached the Parlour. Walpole, ever the gourmand, came up with a wonderful solution. He had Kent build a free-standing fireplace, which concealed a door in the rear wall. The servants would enter the room unseen and serve the food through a pair of marble arches either side of the fireplace. Hot food, however, would be placed onto lead-lined shelves into a cupboard at the rear of the fireplace, where the heat of the fire would keep it warm until required.

Meanwhile, two tables at the back of the room were fitted with pipes and taps which enabled water to be pumped up to the Parlour and drawn off from a supply provided by the nearby water tower. The water was run off into a pair of large Roman marble bowls and would be used for rinsing and washing, and also for the cooling of wine and beer bottles. For the early part of the 18th century, this proved to be quite a revolutionary arrangement. Water required for the rest of the 'piano nobile' level or higher would still need to be carried in buckets and pails.

An example of the class system of the time can be clearly seen halfway along the north side of the state apartments. Between the Embroidered Bedchamber and the Tapestry Dressing Room lies a small servants' lobby. At no time would a guest enter this lobby. They would progress to their required destinations via the state rooms alone. As a result, the lobby is bare, and, like the family's side of the house, has a plain ceiling and no gilding on the outside of the doors. The other side of the doors are gilded, and the ceilings painted. Yet another example of Walpole's reluctance to waste money on an area that would not be viewed by those who mattered.

The most curious and intriguing of all the house's curiosities must surely be the Great Staircase. Here, with Kent's connivance, Walpole excelled himself. The staircase is situated on the south side, running up through the private part of the house. Originally, long before his infamous grandson disposed of the exterior steps, it was never intended that the staircase would be used by guests. They would only be able to view its awesome majesty through a door frame that led from the Stone Hall onto the first floor landing.

Walpole, apparently short of cash after the cost of the Stone Hall, decided on a piece of artistic trickery to fool his guests. Knowing he couldn't afford the cost of a stone-walled stair, he arranged for Kent to paint the brilliant piece of 'trompe l'oeil', executed in 'grisaille' on canvas board on all four walls. It depicted scenes from the story of Meleager and Atalanta. The stairwell was intended to resemble the principle of an Italian courtyard, and light was provided by the glassed roof at the top of the house. Around the stairwell was a grand cantilevered stone staircase, the steps being set deep into the walls. A balustrade of finely carved mahogany surrounded the steps.

And rising up through the centre of the space, from ground to first floor level, was a temple-like plinth on which stood a dramatic copy of the Borghese 'Gladiator'. The original Gladiator had been discovered in 1611 at Nettuno, near Anzio, and entered the Borghese Collection in Rome in 1613. In 1807, it was bought by Napoleon Bonaparte. Shortly after its discovery, copies were made. The 8th Earl of Pembroke,* having one such a copy for his gardens at Wilton House in Wiltshire, gave his friend, Sir Robert Walpole, the present of a second copy, designed by Le Sueur, for Houghton. Rather than place his in the gardens, Walpole deliberately arranged for it to become the focal point of his amazing staircase.

With its installation, Walpole's masterpiece of illusion was complete. Guests looking through the door from the Stone Hall would, by flickering candlelight, see the Gladiator and the mass of mahogany in the balustrade and think they were looking at real stone walls rather than painted canvas. Such was the skill employed by Kent, that painted busts throwing painted shadows in painted alcoves still look like the real thing after almost 300 years.

Though William Kent must, quite rightly, be given the lion's share of the credit for Houghton's interior design, the work of his equally talented cohorts in craftsmanship, Giuseppe Artari and John Michael Rysbrack, should not be overlooked.

Rysbrack's magnificent bust of Walpole stands proudly above the fireplace in the Stone Hall. It brilliantly captures the arrogance and self-assuredness of its sitter, as well as displaying the man's obvious vanity. We see Walpole in the toga of a Roman senator, and, in place of his usual wig, he sports a typical Caesar-like hairstyle. Around the walls stand the busts of real Romans - relics of Grand Tours - all at a slightly lower level than Walpole. The inference is clear. Not only did Walpole and the early Georgian politicians see themselves as the new Caesars, they considered themselves better than the originals. And to compound this vanity, a closer examination of Walpole's toga will show the Garter Star carved into its folds. Walpole was immensely proud of this honour, and here was yet another place to display it.

But Rysbrack's greatest achievement at Houghton must surely be his finely crafted over mantle in the Marble Parlour. 'The Sacrifice to Bacchus' depicts a central figure about to slaughter a tied ram, while a bull and a goat are being readied as the next victims. The carving was cut from one solid piece of stone, with

* Lord Pembroke was Groom of the Stole to King George II

Rysbrack working downwards to display a tremendous feeling of perspective. The base - on which animals and humans stand – is roughly hewn to resemble rocky ground, but, as the eye is taken into the piece, the different layers of fine carving and detail become apparent.

The left arm of the slaughterer appears, at first glance, to be solid and part of the whole. On closer examination the viewer realises that one's fingers can be slipped behind the arm and out the other side. One can only speculate at the time, patience and great care it must have taken to perform this feat without damaging the delicate features of the arm itself. The slightest slip would have proved fatal.

Artari was a splendid exponent of the plasterer and stuccoist's trade. His work at Houghton speaks for itself, but special mention should be made of the lines of plump little 'putti' or cherubs which line the walls of the Stone Hall. We are assured that all of them - even those with their backs to us – are all little boys, with the clear exception of one who is very definitely a little girl. The generally accepted story is that she was put there by the workmen for Sir Robert's amusement. Is it just a coincidence that the eyes of Walpole's bust appear to look directly up at this angelic little cherub, or was this a clear intention of collusion between Rysbrack and Artari to perpetuate the workmen's joke?

While the ceilings, carvings and sculptures – due mainly to their size - tend to dominate, there is another important aspect of the craftsmen's art that should not be overlooked. The full range of mouldings, so definitive of the Palladian style, are all in evidence on the 'piano nobile' at Houghton. The Acanthus Leaf and Bay Leaf Garland feature prominently. The former, resurrected from an ancient and popular motif, is based on the toothed and jagged leaf of the acanthus plant. The Garland displays a horizontal band of formal bay leaves with a criss-cross binding at regular intervals.

The lesser mouldings include:-

Dentil – 3 dimensional teeth-like (hence the derivation) blocks, clearly separated from one another;
Egg-and-Dart – ovoid shapes alternating with vertical arrow or spearheads (sometimes known as Egg-and-Tongue);
Greek Key or Meander - an angular, maze-like pattern of which there are a number of variants;
Vitruvian Wave or Scrolls - a flowing pattern of curvilinear lines;
Bead-and-Reel - a sequence of alternating round and oblong shapes.

Surprisingly, it is this latter moulding, simplest of all the types, that is shown off to best effect at Houghton. In a very short space between the Great Staircase and the Common Parlour, the Bead-and-Reel is presented in four clear and distinct forms, showing not only the versatility of the craftsmen and artists but the continuing need to preserve, yet again, the essential balance so vital to the Palladian style. Thus, flowing continuity is allowed to prevail.

Looking like an early Georgian Morse Code, it begins with dots and dashes painted onto the canvas 'trompe l'oeil'. Within inches it is reprised in carved stone on the door frame, then in mahogany on the door casing and, finally, in lesser wood and painted over, on the dado rail of the Parlour.

Another important aspect of the house was its lighting requirements. Most of the larger rooms had chandeliers, usually of a metal design and not particularly artistic in their construction. Some of these operated by means of a rope and pulley system. At a lower level, candelabra were moved around alcoves and tables as desired. A house like Houghton would have used the most refined candles available, thus reducing but certainly not removing the problem of smoke and soot deposit.

Records tell us that the original chandelier in the Stone Hall was a 'hideous lantern shaped affair', big enough for a man to stand inside. Sadly, no drawings of this seem to survive, and it was replaced in 1748, three years after Walpole's death, by the gilded wooden chandelier that now hangs in the Hall, and came from one of the Cholmondeley's London properties. It is ironic that today, thanks to the benefit of skilfully placed concealed electric lighting, we can see the beautiful ceilings of both the Marble Parlour and the Saloon to far better effect than the original occupants did in the 18th century. The most interesting and beautiful of Houghton's chandeliers, a magnificent creation of English crystal, would not be added to the house until 1805.

The only other illumination in the house would come from the large fireplaces with their roaring wood fires. Despite their obvious grandeur, these fireplaces were rather inadequate with much of the heat going up the chimneys. Such large rooms were often cold in winter, and this meant people had to sit quite close to the fires, hence the need for fire screens. These prevented the ladies from fainting due to the heat or risking their heavy make-up from running.

Outside the house, lighting in the evenings would have been provided by brands and torches, enabling guests to walk in the gardens or to be shown to their carriages.

With each new section of the house being completed, it now fell to Walpole to organise the interior decoration to his own particular taste. The walls were decorated in a variety of tapestries and hangings. Many walls hung with a rich, dark green velvet, the most expensive velvet available at the time, and it reflected the position and wealth of those who used it. Green was considered to be the colour of Venus. As there was no natural green dye, the colour was made up of blue and yellow dyes. Arsenic was also used in the colouring process, and this would have a ruinous effect on the fabric over a period of time.

The walls of the Saloon were hung in an equally rich red Utrecht velvet called Caffoy. This was a wool fabric which imitated silk, and had a linen warp with a goat hair pile. It was also usable for upholstery, as witnessed by the matching saloon chairs in the room. When it was hung, it had cost the princely sum of 14/6d (almost 75p) a yard.

Green Velvet Bedchamber, Houghton. © Houghton Hall.

Pediment, West Front, Houghton. Statues left to right Justice, Desmosthenes, Minerva. © Houghton Hall.

The Green Velvet Bedchamber boasted the only tapestries exclusively designed for the house. Made in Brussels, they were based on designs by Albano and depicted scenes from the life of Venus and Adonis and Venus and Vulcan. The Embroidered Bedchamber was hung with impressive Brussels tapestries showing 'The Taking of Dionysus from Naxos' and 'The Marriage of Dionysus to Ariadne'.

The most exciting of the tapestries, however, were the ones depicting the Stuarts, which took pride of place on the walls of the dressing room attached to the first state bedroom. In Walpole's time, this was known as the Van Dyck Dressing Room. Woven by Francis Poyntz at Mortlake, and dated 1672, they were based on Stuart portraits and show the figures of James I, his wife Anne of Denmark, Charles I, his wife Henrietta Maria and Christian IV of Denmark, the brother of Anne. Woven pilaster strips contain medallions of Stuart children, although one of these is blank, in memory of a child believed stillborn.

It is said that Walpole inherited these unique tapestries, but one feels there must be more to it than than that. Walpole was a staunch Hanoverian supporter, and the Hanoverians had no love for the Stuarts. It can be assumed that the tapestries, no longer required for the royal palaces, were to have been disposed of in some way. Walpole, who had both a fine eye for art and a bargain, somehow managed to obtain the tapestries and brought them to the old manor house at Houghton, intending to hang them in the dressing room once it had been completed. It seems strange that Walpole, so loyal to his new masters, should dare to hang the portraits of the former monarchy in his new house, but who would dare to take the most powerful politician to task over such an issue!

Another requirement for the Hall was the provision of furniture, and it fell to William Kent to design most of the items needed, including a mixture of green and red seating. The most attractive green chairs, however, were those combining burr-walnut and gilded gesso in their construction, and attributed to the Roberts family. They date from the earlier part of the 18th century and were probably ordered by Sir Robert when he altered the old house about 1715-16. Eventually being transferred to the new Hall, they were then recovered in the expensive green fabric. In their new location, they were placed in what were then known as the 'Cabinett and Cov'd or Wrought Bedchamber'.

The Saloon contained a particularly fine set of seat furniture designed by Kent. Today, the visitor can see a pair of settees, twelve armchairs and two stools, all of which were probably made at Houghton by James Richards, the principal Office of Works carver, and one of Kent's favourite craftsmen. Well known to Thomas Ripley, he is recorded as being at Houghton in 1726 and 1729. The furniture is covered in the same Caffoy fabric which adorns the walls. A true saloon chair would normally have a plain back, the intention being that the seat would usually be placed against a wall and rarely moved. The unique red chairs at Houghton were intended to be moved around the room in whatever configuration was required at the time. As a result, the backs of the chairs carry the overall pattern of the fronts, but in a much lighter and faded tone.

The larger rooms featured a variety of pier tables, several of them carrying the Walpole coat of arms, or the Saracen's Head. After Walpole was made a Knight of the Garter in 1726, the Garter star appeared on several items of furniture, which was to prove a useful guide in dating items as pre or post 1726.

Another fine piece was Sir Robert's dining table in the Marble Parlour. It stood at its full length of 16 feet (4.9 metres), boasting a total of 32 legs, but could be reduced in size by removing its leaves, dependent on the number of persons dining at the time.

Walpole filled his two state bedrooms with a pair of fine beds, both about seventeen feet high. The second state bed was hung with oriental needlework based on a mixture of oriental and chinoiserie designs. The presence of the Garter on the coat of arms of the headcloth and the corners of the canopy show the bed must have been ordered after 1726, but it was ready for use as the state bed when the Duke of Lorraine visited Houghton in 1731.

But it is William Kent's spectacular green velvet bed which really deserves attention. The lush green velvet drapes were originally protected by a set of muslin over-curtains, which eventually rotted and were removed. The bed boasts the huge shell of Venus on its headcloth, relating to the scenes of the goddess on Albano's adjacent tapestries. The gold and silver trimmings, now looking somewhat black and distressed in places, cost a staggering £1,219-3s-11d.

The importance of this sum is appreciated when one learns that this is only one of a few bills that survives for the building, decoration and furnishing of Houghton. Knowing that he was to be the subject of a possible corruption investigation, Walpole sent a messenger from Westminster to Houghton with an order to the head steward to burn all the bills. The bill for the trimmings was one of the few items to evade the conflagration, and must, therefore, be used as a yardstick in calculating the possible cost of the house and its contents. It has been estimated that the bed alone cost in the region of £20,000. When pressed by a neighbour, Walpole had claimed his new home had cost about £200,000. This, however, would have been a blatant lie, as Walpole attempted to evade the issue of the real cost. On the strength of building Houghton alone, the richest and most powerful politician in England would die passing on a debt of over £40,000 to his son and heir.

Of much interest to visitors today is the whereabouts of the toilets and bathrooms. Such things didn't exist to any large degree in Walpole's day, the occupants relying on discreetly placed commodes and chamber pots. Bathing was an occasional and sparing extravagance, with what little washing there was being done with the aid of water jugs, basins and hip baths. The Georgians were often somewhat lacking in personal hygiene, relying on pot-pourri or vinaigrettes to mask unpleasant odours. Walpole, however, had the personal luxury of a bath on his side of the house.

Sir Robert now filled the house with his fine and burgeoning art collection, which was said to have cost him in the region of £40,000, and which he began amassing in 1717. It included some of the finest works of Van Dyck, Rubens, Rembrandt, Raphael, Teniers, Claude Lorraine, Paul Veronese, Titian, Poussin, Sir Godfrey Kneller and Carlo Maratti among others.

The pictures, in their heavy frames, were often hung directly onto the green velvet wall hangings. In the cabinet alone, 51 of his favourite smaller pictures adorned the walls. It was only when his infamous grandson, George, was to sell many of the pictures some fifty years later that the velvet on the walls had to be removed. The pictures and their frames had greatly distressed, torn and faded the hangings. All 51 of the pictures in the Cabinet would be among the 204 that George would happily sell to Catherine the Great for £40,555. Allowing for the quality of the artwork on the walls, George made no profit on his grandfather's original investment.

Almost every picture is worth a mention in its own right, but I have singled out one in particular. Originally hanging over the fireplace in the Common Parlour was a stunningly crafted portrait of the woodcarver and sculptor Grinling Gibbons, an oil on canvas painted by Sir Godfrey Kneller in the 1680s. Horace Walpole would comment about Kneller that he *"... has shown himself as great in that portrait as the man who sat to him"*. It must have looked magnificent in its space above the fireplace, especially considering that it was framed by an exquisitely carved garland of pear-tree wood done by Gibbons, which is still 'in situ' today. The carving had originally been located in the old manor house, and Walpole had it transferred to the Hall to act as a fine and imposing extra frame to Gibbons' portrait. Sadly, the portrait now hangs, along with many others in the great sale, in The Hermitage in St. Petersburg.

In addition to the great paintings, Walpole had also invested in fine paintings of the family. Of special note were the portraits of himself – striking a pose with tricorn and dogs as the Warden of Richmond Park, painted by John Wootton; as the Chancellor of the Exchequer in Jean Baptiste Van Loo's fine canvass; and in his Garter robes, after Jonathan Richardson. Walpole was always pictured as the middle-aged politician or elder statesman, so it is refreshing to see him as a 35-year-old politician on the rise as Secretary At War in Charles Jervais's portrait. Other notable portraits include both his wives, Catherine Shorter and Maria Skerret, painted respectively by Michael Dahl and Van Loo. But the finest portrayals come from the talented hand of the female Italian artist Rosalba Carriera. Her pastels of Walpole's three sons were all done on the various Grand Tours the young gentlemen undertook, and were brought home to Houghton as presents for their father. The expertise and consistency of the works make them all appear to have been done at the same sitting, whereas Robert's was done in 1722-23, Edward's about 1730 and Horace's being completed in 1741.

Another fine example of interior decoration came in the form of a copy of the classic Laocoon, which stands in the Stone Hall on a stone plinth created by Kent. The bronze sculpture, based on the original in the Vatican, was commissioned in Paris by Walpole's brother, Horatio, when the latter was Sir Robert's Ambassador to Paris. The work was created about 1690 by J.J. and J.B. Keller under the supervision of Francois Giradon (1628-1715).

With the construction of the house well under way, the other new features of the estate began to take shape. As early as 1707, Sir Robert had already begun to plant trees, and, about 1715-16, he laid out a new parterre on the west side of the old house. This was to help in determining the placing of the new house when he was ready to commence building in 1722. A relatively small estate of some 225 acres (91 hectares) was gradually increased to form a park and plantations that was 6 miles (10 kilometres) round, and had a herd of 1,500 fallow deer as well as 200 pheasants being raised every year. The noted landscape gardener Charles Bridgeman was engaged to lay out the estate's plantations.

Walpole realised that the old village of Houghton, with its higgledy-piggledy hotchpotch of wattle-and-daub cottages and an old inn, 'The Dun Cow', lay too close to the Hall and would seriously detract from the view. He decided to pull down the village and rebuild it in the form of a series of white cottages and a main street outside the park. This was also a good opportunity to get rid of some of the less desirable characters and drunks who had taken advantage of the old location. The villagers would also benefit from the gift of fruit trees. The centre of the old village would be commemorated by a stone pillar, which, though worn, still stands to this day.

On 4th July 1729, the foundation was dug for the first two houses of the new village, which was variously called Houghton-le-Brake, Houghton-in-the-Brake or New Houghton, the latter being the name it is known by today. The resiting of the village has always been held as the inspiration for Oliver Goldsmith to write his poem, "The Deserted Village", which was published in May 1770.

To the north west of the new house, Walpole built the Water Tower between 1731 and 1733. It was designed by Lord Herbert, who became 9th Earl of Pembroke in 1733. It is at the end of the avenue aligned on the West Front parterre. It was constructed of stuccoed brick, and incorporated a three-bay facade with slender Tuscan pilasters. The ground floor was rusticated with arches.

St. Martin's Church, Houghton. © Houghton Hall.

The medieval church of St Martin's stood to the southwest and had been enlarged and restored over the centuries. In 1730, Sir Robert decided to rebuild the tower as a memorial to his grandfather, Sir Jeffry Burwell. Sir Robert's decision to combine Gothic and classic designs in the rebuild probably came from his acquaintance with London churches in a similar style.

After the Hall, it is the fine stable block which architecturally most impresses the visitor today. It is attributed to William Kent, and was erected between 1733 and 1735. In his capacity as an architect, Kent had already built the Royal Mews in London from 1731 to 1733. The Square, as it is known, was built with local carrstone on the outside and brick on the inside walls. Magnificently constructed red brick vaulting was supported by stout timber pillars. It takes the form of a large quadrangle with lunette-shaped windows and polygonal turrets. It was large enough to house 80 horses of varying qualities at any one time. The most valuable mounts were kept in individual stalls, coach horses sharing stalls, with partitions for every other horse. Accommodation for the grooms was provided in the rooms above the stalls. Immediately adjacent to the stables was a large dung yard.

With the exception of the unfinished chapel, the new Hall was, after thirteen years of construction, finally completed in 1735.

Or was it?

Not immediately obvious, a thin, decorated stone frieze runs around the top of the outside walls of the house. It is easily overlooked because of a bolder tongue and dart frieze situated slightly below it. The frieze runs along the south side and down the east and west fronts, before turning at right angles to join the north side. It runs for a few feet at either end of the north wall before suddenly stopping, failing to join up in the middle section of the wall.

A tax was due on all completed buildings. By failing to allow the joining up of the frieze, Walpole could legitimately claim his new house was unfinished, thus exempting himself from the duty payable!

With his new mansion approaching completion, Walpole wasted no time in introducing its glories and grandeur to his friends.

11
CONGRESSES AND CABINETS

Renowned for his hospitality as a host, Walpole now had a venue where he could entertain and impress in style. Houghton became the Chequers of its day. A grand country retreat, it combined the opportunities for business and pleasure, allowing Walpole every chance to reward and retain existing supporters, while endeavouring to win over new converts to his causes.

His celebrated Norfolk Congresses became regular events in the country calendar, held over several days in summer and winter. In addition to his special visits to Norfolk, whenever time and political duties allowed, he went up to Norfolk twice a year – for ten days in the summer, and twenty days each November. He would travel from London to Houghton by coach, a journey which took three days, with two nights on the road, stopping off at suitable coaching inns or at the homes of friends en route. He would usually travel with a document chest so that he could work on his political papers during the journey and stopovers.

At the small market town of Swaffham, he would be met by Sturge, his Norfolk runner, who was a Houghton man. "Dressed in flannel and belted", Sturge would run, a lighted torch in his hand, in front of his master's carriage, all the way to Houghton, a distance of some fifteen miles. Walpole would often encourage his travelling companions to bet on Sturge's ability to cover the ground and the time it would take him.

Arriving at Houghton, his guests would always be greeted in style from the moment they alighted from their carriages, ascended the East Front stairs and entered into the magnificent space of the Stone Hall. Both at the old manor house and in the new Hall, Walpole knew the importance of having good and reliable staff to attend to the needs of himself and his guests. He liked to have his chosen, trusted experts about him. These included his head chef, Solomon Sollis; his butler, Grantham; and his personal footman, Harry Yardley. A reliable head steward was vital for the smooth running of a large country house, especially when the owner was, like Walpole, away from the property for any considerable time. He had an excellent man in John Wrott, who sadly died in 1720. His replacement was the equally efficient James Rolfe. Walpole also had a trusted gardener in Fulke Harold, so highly regarded that he even had his portrait painted.

A typical Congress day would begin with two sessions of hunting, split between the morning and afternoon by an informal lunch in the ground floor Arcade. This would allow the grooms time to prepare remounts for the afternoon. Walpole was believed to have sometimes ridden a horse that had once belonged to the Old Pretender, James Francis Edward Stuart.*

* Attributed to The Rev John H. Broome, Vicar at Houghton – 1865

57

The Arcade was the family's entrance to the hall and was the longest room within the house, reaching from the East Front to the West. Low vaulted, pillared and dark, it was big enough to accommodate four large fireplaces in its length. Settles would be lodged between the pillars in front of the fires, and here Walpole and his guests, exhausted from a morning's hard riding, would lounge, dogs at their feet, enjoying a luncheon of cold meats washed down with a potent local beer called Hogan, which was brewed on the estate.

In the evening, the guests would sit down to dine in style in the splendour of the Marble Parlour. The following extract from Lord John Hervey's diary gives a fine description of the festivities. *"Our company at Houghton swelled at last into so numerous a party that we used to sit down to dinner a little snug party of about thirty odd, up to the chin in beef, venison, geese, turkeys, etc; and generally over the chin in claret, strong beer and punch. We had Lords spiritual and temporal, besides commoners, parsons and freeholders innumerable. In public we drank loyal healths, talked of the times and cultivated popularity: in private we drew plans and cultivated the country."*

The scale of Walpole's hospitality and his love of good wines can be gathered from his purchases of Château Margaux and Château Lafite by the hogshead, his expenditure of £1,118 with one wine merchant in 1733 and his return of 522 dozen (6,264) empty bottles to the same man.

Already well sated, Walpole and his guests would then adjourn to the Cabinet where, over pipes and port, they would proceed to discuss business, politics, affairs of state, gossip and scandal until the small hours. Always attuned to every nuance, Walpole played the perfect host while keeping his finger firmly on the political pulse of such discussions.

No matter what they may have thought of Walpole as a man, few of his visitors could have failed to have been impressed by his house and hospitality. There were some, however, who were somewhat less than complimentary in their views.

Lord Oxford was most definitely unimpressed with Houghton, though one feels this was due to his opposition to the man rather than his property.

"This house," he wrote, *"has made a great deal of noise, but I think it is not deserving of it. Some admire it because it belongs to the first Minister: others envy it because it is his, and consequently rail at it. These gentlemen's praise and blame are not worth anything, because they know nothing of the art of building, or anything about it. I think it is neither magnificent nor beautiful, there is very great expense without either judgment or taste."*

He thought Colen Campbell *"an ignorant rascal"* and said *"...in the house as it is now is a composition of the greatest blockheads and most ignorant fellows in architect that are."*

He considered the hanging of the pictures in the saloon all wrong. The Stone Hall was overcrowded with terms and busts and far too dark. The quality of mahogany used in the doors revealed *"...the greatest profusion and waste."* And the rooms on the ground floor had a *"very ill look."* As for the gardens, he added, *"...we did not go into them, we saw enough of them from the window."*

The poet and satirist Alexander Pope had an equally poor opinion of Thomas Ripley and his work at Houghton when he wrote:-

"Heaven visits with a taste the wealthy fool,
And needs no rod but Ripley with a rule."

and

"So Ripley, till his destined space is filled,
Heaps bricks on bricks, and fancies 'tis to build."

Lord Hervey, however, had somewhat mixed feelings. Following his visit to the house in the summer of 1731, he confided to his diary Townshend's anguish at seeing Houghton's rise, referring to the Hall as *"this fabric of fraternal discord"* and remarking that Townshend *"...considered every stone that augmented the splendour of Houghton as a diminuation of the grandeur of Raynham."*

Referring to the flatness of the Houghton countryside, Hervey wrote, *"the soil is not fruitful here, there is little wood and no water...These are disadvantages he [Walpole] had to struggle with, when that natural leaning to the paternal field and the scene of his youth, a bias which everybody feels and nobody can account for, determined him to adorn and settle at Houghton. He has already, by the force of manuring and planting, so changed the face of the county, that his park is a pleasant, fertile island of his own creation in the middle of a naked sea of land."*

Hervey referred to The Arcade as *"...the base or rustic story"* and *"...that the whole is dedicated to foxhunters, hospitality, noise , dirt and business."*

Of the 'piano nobile' he said it *"...is the floor of taste, expense, state and parade,"* and that the stucco work in the Stone Hall had surpassed anything he had seen in the country.

In conclusion he observed, *"The great staircase is the greatest, cheerfullest and prettiest thing I ever saw; some very beautiful heresies in the particulars, and the result of the whole more charming than any bigotry I ever saw."*

The last word, however, should go to Sir Thomas Robinson of Rokeby, whose enthusiasm for Houghton was almost unbounded. He believed *"...it is the best house in the world for its size, capable of the greatest reception for company, and the most convenient state apartments, very noble, especially the hall and saloon."*

He continued, *"The finishing of the inside is, I think, a pattern for all great houses that may hereafter be built..."*

Robinson was much in favour of the offices, stables, gardens and park. He had apparently tried to persuade Sir Robert to build his new stables as wings to the east front of the house, but Walpole preferred a more detached quadrangle at some distance from the house.

According to Robinson, there were to be *"plumps and avenues to go quite round the park pale, and to make straight and oblique lines of a mile or two in length, as the situation of the country admits of. This design will be about twelve miles in circumference, and nature has disposed of the country so as these plantations will have a very noble and fine effect; and at every angle there are to be obelisks, or some other building."* Walpole, however, dispensed with any idea of erecting obelisks.

"In short," wrote Robinson, *"the out works at Houghton will be 200 years hence what those at Castle Howard are now, for he has very little full-grown timber, and not a drop of water for ornament; but take all together, it is a seat so perfectly magnificent and agreeable, that I think nothing but envy itself can find fault because there is no more of the one, and I scarce missed the entire of the other."*

Without doubt, Houghton Hall stands as a proud and lasting monument to its creator, Sir Robert Walpole.

12
MAD GEORGE

After Sir Robert and Horace, George, 3rd Earl of Orford, must surely be the most interesting and intriguing of the Walpole clan. A true eccentric in the great British tradition, he would leave his mark on Houghton in a way that would have appalled his illustrious grandfather and certainly horrified his academic uncle.

George, born in 1730, was the son of Robert Walpole, 2nd Earl of Orford, and his wife, Margaret Rolle. His godparents or 'sponsors' were the King and Queen of England. Robert's younger brother, Horace, had no love for his sister-in-law and, in 1742, after taking the boy to Vauxhall, wrote that he found him *"...a most charming boy, but grown excessively like his mother in the face."*

He was even more cutting after her death, when he referred to George as *"...the late Countess's most doubtful son."* This was a clear reference to the rumours that the boy had been fathered by Margaret's lover, Sir George Oxenden.

George, a good looking boy, went to Eton. As he grew up, it was clear that he was developing into a irresponsible and wild young man. When his father died in March 1751, he inherited the estate at Houghton and the title of 3rd Earl. He also inherited a raft of debts handed down to him from the previous two generations. By now, however, the imprudent George was also incurring new and mounting debts of his own.

It was clear quite early on that George was unstable, verging, at times, between mild eccentricity and seeming madness. At other times he was quite capable of acting perfectly normally. This condition was not unlike that of King George III's porphyria and would probably have been easily controlled today with the application of modern drugs. Understandably for the times, but somewhat cruelly, George earned himself the nickname of 'Mad George'.

A keen and competitive sportsman, he was, however, a terrible and incessant gambler. Such was his constant misfortune at the gaming tables or the racecourse that his inherited debts were already rising with the accumulation of his own gambling losses. His condition and predicament worried his uncle Horace who tried to arrange a marriage for the young man with a rich heiress called Margaret Nicoll. It was Horace's hope that this would help to steady the boy and bring him some financial solvency. Miss Nicoll agreed to the arrangement, but George refused to marry her. She would eventually marry Lord Camarthen.

As the debts began to rise, so Houghton began to fall into disrepair as a result of George's combined lack of funds and peculiar behaviour. Horace was greatly alarmed but felt there was very little he could do for his nephew. He wrote of George, *"He talks of selling Houghton with a coolness that wants nothing but being intended for philosophy to be the greatest that ever was."*

Warming to his theme, Horace continued, *"He is the most selfish man in the world, without being the least interested: he loves nobody but himself, yet neglects every view of fortune or ambition..."*

"He drinks without inclination; has women, not without inclination, but without having them, for he brags as much as an old man: games without attention; is immeasurably obstinate..."

But, despite George's wild and impulsive behaviour, Horace still clearly had a soft spot for the young man. *"In short, it is impossible not to love him when one sees him..."*

George loved rural pursuits and spent most of his time in the country indulging his passion for all forms of sport. His main loves were for hunting and racing, coursing, hawking, cock-fighting and bull-baiting. His gambling, however, was getting out of control as he delighted in making even more preposterous wagers. In December 1756, he challenged Lord Rockingham to race five turkeys against five geese from Norwich to London. The stakes were agreed at £500, and the winner would be the man with the least losses. Sadly, history does not record the result of the wager.

His eccentricity was clearly demonstrated by his fashion of driving in a phaeton pulled by four red deer through the streets of Newmarket, where he was a frequent visitor for the races. On one occasion he was pursued by a pack of hounds which had caught the scent of the deer. The frightened animals bolted through the town and George was able to head them in the direction of a local inn, 'The Ram'. As George, deer and carriage clattered into the inn's courtyard, ostlers were luckily on hand to shut the gates against the hounds just in time!

In 1755 George was appointed a Lord of the Bedchamber, and, in 1757, succeeded the 1st Earl of Buckinghamshire as Lord Lieutenant of Norfolk. In this post he played a leading role in raising, organising and drilling the troops of the Norfolk Militia, reminiscent of his great grandfather, Colonel Robert. George was responsible for helping to bring the Militia to a very high standard of efficiency. About this time he also accepted an appointment as High Steward of Great Yarmouth.

He then applied for and was offered the position of Minister of Turin in 1758, but promptly declined the post. This was probably just as well, because he, of all men, was hardly suited to a diplomatic career.

Following the death of King George II in 1760 and an impending general election, George asked Horace to visit him in Norfolk. Horace suggested it would be better for George to remain in London and take his part as a peer and Lord of the Bedchamber in the forthcoming funeral ceremonies.

After the election, with Horace returned to office, uncle and nephew left London for Houghton.

George, however, stopped off en route at Newmarket for the racing, thus failing to act as a host to his uncle who travelled up to Norfolk alone.

When Henry Fox, the Government leader in the Commons, tried to rally support for John Bute's unpopular anti-Whig administration, he offered the post of the Rangership of St. James's and Hyde Parks – at a cost of £2,200 a year – to George, in return for Orford's support and that of Charles Boone, George's nominated member for Castle Rising. With his uncle acting as a go-between, George readily accepted the post and the welcome income. He never repaid the Ministry, failing to attend the House of Lords and never casting a single vote on the Government's behalf.

He preferred to remain in the country, where his increasing extravagances and behaviour continued to alarm Horace. By now he had also taken up with a group of friends that Horace thought undesirable, referring to them as *"a rookery of harpies"*.

George had taken himself a mistress, Mrs Patty Turk, a striking beauty who had once been a maidservant at Houghton. George was smitten with her, and she proved to be one of the better and more stabilising influences on his life. The couple were devoted to each other and she frequently presided over his table at Houghton with grace and charm. They also spent long periods of relaxation at a vicarage-style house at Eriswell, between Brandon and Newmarket, which enabled George easy access to the racecourse at Newmarket.

But several of George's new friends proved unworthy, taking advantage of him and his position. They encouraged him in his wild ways while happily spending his money.

In 1773, George was taken seriously ill while staying at an inn on the Newmarket road. His mental condition had worsened and it again fell to Horace, as his only caring relative, to try and sort out George's affairs. Horace was horrified to discover just how bad things had become at Houghton, which had developed into a state of alarming ruination.

He wrote : - *"The two great staircases exposed to all weathers, every room in the wings rotting with wet, the ceiling of the gallery in danger, the chancel of the church unroofed, the waterhouse built by Lord Pembroke tumbling down, the garden a common, the park half covered with nettles and weeds, the walls and pales in ruin, perpetuities of livings at the very gates sold, the interest of Lynn gone, mortgages swallowing the estate, and a debt of above £40,000 heaped on those of my father and brother."*

"A crew of banditti were harboured in the house, stables, town and every adjacent tenement..."

Horace, despite the fact that he had never really appreciated his father's house, set to with a will to rectify the situation, and managed to get the great estate of Houghton back on a reasonably sound footing.

Suddenly, as quickly as he had lost it, George regained his reason, much to Horace's relief. George was duly grateful and seemed to have reformed. But it didn't last, and he was soon back to his old ways, gambling and spending as wildly as ever. Horace, understandably, had had enough and wisely returned to Strawberry Hill.

The summer of 1773 was a bad time for George, as his mental condition lapsed once more, but, by the following summer, he was back to normal again. He spent the summer of 1774 making a three week voyage through The Fens in the company of Patty Turk and two young friends, William Roberts and George Farington. By all accounts, it was a happy and enjoyable trip.

In his more lucid moments, George was never happier than following a range of country pursuits. His main passion was coursing, and he organised various clubs and societies to follow the sport. Coursing is defined as the pursuit of game by hounds hunting by sight and not by scent. In 1776, George became regarded as the father of modern coursing when he established the Swaffham Coursing Club, which would become a model for many others clubs to follow. The Club's meetings, held at nearby Westacre, were well attended. Membership was originally restricted to between 20 and 30 persons, with each member being allotted a letter of the alphabet and a colour, and meeting twice a year at first. Once a member had been assigned a letter, all his dogs had to have names beginning with that letter. To begin with, the running had consisted almost entirely of matches, but subsequently a £50 Challenge Cup for 16 greyhounds on knock-out lines became the premier stake. The Swaffham Club boasted many respected patrons, including the Ladies Cholmondeley and Townshend. In 1776, following George's establishment of the Club, the first written code for greyhound coursing was made by the Duke of Norfolk.

George, who had a hundred greyhounds in his kennels, experimented in breeding and cross-breeding for the sport, and is thought to have been the first breeder to introduce the bulldog cross from which the brindle colour is supposed to stem.

Another of George's passions was hawking, and, in 1772, he became the President of a renowned falconers' society known as The Confederate Hawks of Great Britain.

In April 1777, Orford was taken seriously ill again with a new bout of insanity. Horace came to his aid once more, arranging for physicians to attend his nephew's alarming condition. The attack would last for almost a year, when George suddenly snapped back to normality once more. By this time the exhausted and exasperated Horace refused to get involved any further in George's affairs.

When the country went to war, George promptly assumed command of the Norfolk Militia, and alarmed the authorities by ordering the suburbs of Norwich to be burned in the event of the French landing anywhere on the coast. Luckily for Norwich, no such attacks materialised, and George's enthusiasm for his military role eventually abated.

He had promised to pay off his grandfather's long outstanding debts, though just how he planned to do this – in view of his own extravagances and gambling debts – was never quite clear. Neither of his uncles, Edward and Horace, would receive all the money due to them under their father's will. Horace had been bequeathed £5,000 but only received £1,000.

George now committed the first of his two great sins at Houghton when he removed the two grand stone staircases that led up to the 'piano nobile' on the East and West Fronts of the Hall. He claimed that he could no longer afford the upkeep of the steps. Another account, however, tells how he lost them at the gaming tables on the turn of a card. The new owner, apparently intending to ship them to the Continent, had them dismantled. They were placed onto a vessel which promptly sank when it hit bad weather, taking Houghton's staircases with it. For the next two hundred years, the only access for visitors was through the ground floor Arcade. It wasn't until 1973 that Sybil Cholmondeley, 5th Marchioness, erected a set of steps on the West Front as a memorial to her late husband. The new staircase was in the style of Robert Walpole's original flight.

In 1779, in an attempt to reduce his increasing debts, George now decided on another drastic course of action. Negotiating with the agents of the Empress Catherine of Russia, he arranged to sell 204 of his grandfather's masterpieces for the sum of £40,555. On her instructions, Catherine the Great's agents had been scouring Europe to buy treasures for the new art collection at The Hermitage in St. Petersburg. Many of Sir Robert Walpole's finest works, including those of Van Dyke, Rembrandt and Rubens, were crated and sent to Russia. Questions were asked in the House in an attempt to stop the sale, but it was too late. For what had been a mere pittance to the wealthy Catherine, she had obtained one of the finest of British art collections. For George, the money received made a vital contribution in reducing his colossal debts.

To show her gratitude, Catherine had presented Orford with a magnificent portrait of herself, which still proudly hangs in The Saloon at Houghton to this day.

At her request, George supplied the Empress with the rules of coursing, and, pleased with his profitable transaction, promptly named his favourite greyhound bitch Czarina! The dog became one of the notable winners of her day.

Needless to say, Horace and Edward were horrified by George's actions which had left the walls of Houghton so bare.

In 1782, George resigned as Lord of the Bedchamber, and the following year he was dismissed from his duties as the Ranger of the Royal Parks. He was now content to remain in the country, following his rural and sporting activities. When a balloon craze swept the country in 1785, he was a keen participant in the proceedings, although he declined to go aloft himself.

In mid-November 1791, his beloved Patty died suddenly at Eriswell. George, distraught at her death, contracted a severe fever and died at Houghton on 5th December 1791. He was 61. Another account of his death, however, tells how he suffered a fit and fell from his horse while watching Czarina winning a coursing heat! A fortnight after his death, he was buried at Houghton, alongside the coffins of his father and grandfather.

His Uncle Horace, now aged 74, inherited Houghton, taking the title of 4th Earl of Orford. He was faced with the daunting task of trying to restore the Hall and estate to its former glory in the remaining years of his life. Declaring himself to be *"...the poorest Earl in England"*, he said of his errant nephew that he *"...has restored me to my birthright, and I shall call myself obliged to him, and be grateful to his memory."*

13
FROM DUKE TO DOWAGER

With the death of Horace in 1797, the Walpole dynasty at Houghton came to an end. The house now passed to George, 4th Earl and 1st Marquess of Cholmondeley (1749-1827). He was the great grandson of Sir Robert Walpole, his grandmother being Walpole's second daughter, Mary.

Despite the attempts of Horace to address the ravages wreaked on Houghton by his wayward nephew, George, the Hall was still in a poor state of repair. It now fell to the very capable Marquess to continue the work that would make Houghton habitable once more. One of George Cholmondeley's very good friends was the Prince of Wales, who made several visits to Houghton. He apparently slept one night in the green velvet bed, but swore that he would never occupy it again. He was adamant that he had seen the ghost of 'The Brown Lady' – Sir Robert's sister, Dolly – although those not so well disposed towards the Prince would claim he had drunk too much port the night before! Whatever he did or didn't see, the Prince was always provided with alternative sleeping arrangements thereafter.

The experience of seeing a ghost certainly didn't dampen the Prince's enjoyment of Houghton, because he was to make the 1st Marquess the most agreeable present of white brocaded silk hangings and valances which still hang at Houghton today. They were woven at Spitalfields by the Huguenots, and legend tells how the Prince only ordered two sets, one for Houghton, the other for one of the Royal palaces. This having been done, the Prince is then said to have ordered the pattern to be destroyed, never to be repeated.

Eventually, however, it became clear to the Cholmondeleys that the cost of running Houghton was a hopeless cause, and they decided to concentrate on their properties in Cheshire, most notably the magnificent Cholmondeley Castle, a fine creation of the Gothic Medieval. And so the state rooms of Houghton were mostly mothballed, as the house went up for sale. The large windows were blocked off with heavy mahogany shutters and the contents draped in dust sheets, thus preserving the furniture and tapestries for future generations to enjoy and appreciate.

For the best part of ninety years, and the bulk of Queen Victoria's reign, the house remained up for sale. Occasionally, the state rooms would be opened for viewing by prospective purchasers, or for visits by the gentry who indulged in that quaint English version of the European Grand Tour from time to time. But on the south side things were far from quiet. Walpole's former private side of the house and several others rooms were now rented out over the years to a variety of occupants.

One of these was the Reverend John Henry Broome, the vicar of Houghton, who wrote a potted history of Houghton and the Walpoles in 1865. The Rev Broome had been appointed vicar in residence in 1845 by George, 2nd Marquess of Cholmondeley, and remained there until his death in 1887. His son, H.A. Broome, in his memoir "The Log of a Rolling Stone", devoted the first chapter of his book to an account of what happened to Houghton during those years of closure. Young Broome even had the honour, in 1857, of being born in Walpole's library.

The Hall had been offered to the Duke of Wellington by the government, who had offered to purchase the property for him on behalf of a grateful nation, following his victories against Napoleon in the Peninsular and at Waterloo. Wellington is known to have visited the estate on several occasions, and is said to have slept in the green velvet state bed. On his first visit, his arrival was marked by the men of the village who stopped his carriage outside the main gates, unharnessed the horses and then proceeded to pull the carriage the lengthy distance to the entrance at the East Front as a mark of respect.

Wellington is also said to have scratched his name – 'A. Wellington, 1818' – with his keys on one of the pillars of the south colonnade. One feels that if Wellington had done this, he would have been more likely to have scratched 'A. Wellesley'!

Although Wellington liked the estate, the deer park and the opportunities offered for hunting, it was just too far from London to be practical. He already owned Apsley House – No 1 London – and eventually settled on Stratfield Saye as his new home.

Another visitor came to the house in 1851. He was the great nephew of Lord Horatio Nelson, and must have been aware that his illustrious ancestor was descended from the first Prime Minister, Nelson's great great uncle. The nephew, however, was just a journeyman painter. Determined to leave his mark, the nephew scratched his name – 'R. Nelson 1851' – on a pane of glass on the outside of one of the saloon windows, where it is still visible today.

Another prospective buyer for Houghton would be King Edward VII, anxious to buy a Norfolk home for his relaxation. He liked the estate but found the house too big and old in style for his liking, so settled on the nearby property of Sandringham. One of the reasons for his decision was the fact that Sandringham was close to the branch line station of Wolferton. This meant he could travel to King's Lynn and thence to Liverpool Street in London quite quickly. In later years, King George V acquired a large acreage of the Houghton estate to increase and improve the parkland at Sandringham.

Houghton was saved in 1913, when Sybil Sassoon married George Cholmondeley, the Earl of Rocksavage and the gentleman who would, in 1923, become the 5th Marquess. The daughter of Edward Sassoon and Aline de Rothschild, she fell in love with Houghton and decided to make it her future home. She moved to the Hall in 1919, after her husband had returned from service in the Great War, and it was to be her home for the next seventy years until her death, in her 95th year, on Boxing Day, 1989.

She was able to bring the great house back to life, restoring it to its former glory. It is to her great credit that she could, wherever possible, keep it as a memorial to Sir Robert Walpole.

A remarkable woman, she became the friend and confidante of statesmen and monarchs, artists, writers, musicians and sportsmen. She was the originator of the WRNS (the Women's Royal Naval Service), having persuaded the Admiralty that women were perfectly capable of doing shore-based jobs, thus freeing men for sea duty. As a young woman, she delighted in driving Bugatti's, changing to Minis in her later years – which she still drove like Bugatti's!

Her brother was the aesthete and connoisseur, Sir Philip Sassoon, who lived at Trent Park, 13 miles from London. Secretary of State for Air at the Air Ministry, and, later, Commissioner of Works, responsible for the upkeep and decoration of government properties and some royal palaces, he died of pneumonia on 3rd June 1939. With his passing, many of his fine pieces were inherited by his sister and are proudly displayed at Houghton today.

Following the death of her husband in 1968, Sybil's son, Hugh, became the 6th Marquess. He had served in the Royal Dragoons during World War II, when he was awarded the Military Cross, and later transferred to the Grenadier Guards for a further three years after the war. Born in 1919, he began collecting model soldiers in 1928, eventually establishing one of the finest and largest private collections in the world. After the war, he continued building up the collection at Cholmondeley Castle, but, in the 1970s, was persuaded to bring the collection of some 20,000 figures down to Houghton, where it has become a special feature for visitors today.

With Lord Hugh's death in 1990, the estate at Houghton passed to his son, David, who became the 7th Marquess. Inspired by his grandmother, now the Dowager, the new Lord Cholmondeley set about preserving the memory of Sir Robert Walpole, his illustrious ancestor. It is thanks to him that Houghton is, today, a fitting and permanent monument to Great Britain's first Prime Minister.

APPENDIX I

IMPORTANT EVENTS IN THE LIFE OF SIR ROBERT WALPOLE

1676	-	Born at Houghton on 26th August
1700	-	Succeeded to the estate on the death of his father, Col. Robert Walpole
1701	-	Became a Whig MP for Castle Rising
1702	-	Became MP for King's Lynn
1708-1710	-	Secretary At War
1710-1711	-	Treasurer of the Navy
1712	-	Imprisoned in the Tower of London on corruption charges
1714-1717	-	Paymaster General
1715-1717	-	First Lord of the Treasury and Chancellor of the Exchequer
1720	-	The South Sea Bubble scandal
1721	-	First Lord of the Treasury and Chancellor of the Exchequer
1722	-	Foundation stone of Houghton Hall laid on 24th May
1725	-	Created Knight of the Bath
1726	-	Created Knight of the Garter
1735	-	Houghton Hall completed
1737	-	The War of Jenkins's Ear
1742	-	Resigned from the Government and created 1st Earl of Orford
1745	-	Died in London on 18th March. Buried at Houghton.

APPENDIX II
HOUGHTON HALL - SUCCESSION

1	Sir Robert Walpole 1676-1745	-	1st Earl of Orford 1700 - 1745
2	Robert Walpole 1701-1751	-	2nd Earl of Orford 1745- 1751
3	George Walpole 1730-1791	-	3rd Earl of Orford 1751 - 1791
4	Horace Walpole 1717-1797	-	4th Earl of Orford 1791 - 1797

5	George James 1749-1827	-	1st Marquess of Cholmondeley 1797 – 1827
6	George 1792-1870	-	2nd Marquess of Cholmondeley 1827 – 1870
7	William 1800-1894	-	3rd Marquess of Cholmondeley 1870 – 1894
8	George 1858-1923	-	4th Marquess of Cholmondeley 1894 -1923
9	George 1883-1968	-	5th Marquess of Cholmondeley 1923 – 1968
10	Hugh 1919-1990	-	6th Marquess of Cholmondeley 1968-1990
11	David 1960	-	7th Marquess of Cholmondeley 1990

APPENDIX III
SIR ROBERT WALPOLE'S CHILDREN

By Catherine Shorter:-

ROBERT	1701 – 1751
CATHERINE	1703 – 1722
MARY	1704 – 1732
EDWARD	1706 -1784
HORACE	1717 – 1797

By Maria Skerret:-

MARIA	1725 – 1801
CATHERINE	1738 (stillborn)

APPENDIX IV
WALPOLE BURIALS IN ST MARTIN'S CHURCH, HOUGHTON

COFFINS IN THE BURIAL VAULT

1   Sir Robert Walpole

2   Catherine (First wife)

3   Maria (Second wife) and her stillborn child, Catherine

4   Robert (Eldest son and 2nd Earl)

5   Horace (Third son and 4th Earl)

6   George (Grandson and 3rd Earl)

7   Catherine (Daughter)

APPENDIX V
MONARCHS

Sir Robert Walpole lived through the reigns of six monarchs
and served under the last four.

CHARLES II	1630 - 1685
King	1660 -1685
JAMES II	1633 - 1701
King	1685 - 1688
WILLIAM III	1650 - 1702
King	1688 - 1702
ANNE	1665 - 1714
Queen	1702 - 1714
GEORGE I	1660 - 1727
King	1714 - 1727
GEORGE II	1683 - 1760
King	1727 - 1760

APPENDIX VI
THE NELSON CONNECTION

Col Robert Walpole m Mary Burwell

|

Mary   m   Sir Charles Turner

|

Rev Maurice Suckling   m   Anne Turner

|

Catherine Suckling   m   Rev Edmund Nelson

|

Horatio Nelson

Horatio Nelson - 29th September 1758 to 21st October 1805 – was the fifth of eleven children born to the Rev Edmund Nelson and his wife, Catherine Suckling.

Nelson was the great grandson of Mary Walpole, Sir Robert Walpole's sister, and, therefore, the great-great nephew of Sir Robert.

Nelson's uncle was Captain Maurice Suckling RN, and Nelson entered the Royal Navy at the age of 12 under his patronage.

The naval sword of Galfridus Walpole, Sir Robert's brother, was passed to Nelson, his great great nephew.

Nelson was always proud of the fact that he was descended from the first Prime Minister, his great great uncle.

APPENDIX VII
RECOMMENDED READING

Sir Robert Walpole	J.H.Plumb
Walpole	H.T. Dickinson
Walpole In Power	Jeremy Black
Sir Robert Walpole	B.W. Hill
Robert Walpole	G.R. Stirling Taylor
Walpole	John Morley
Bolingbroke and Walpole	Rt Hon J.M. Robertson
Robert Walpole – First 'Prime Minister'	David Yaxley
The Great Man	Edward Pearce
Memoirs and Portraits	Horace Walpole
Life of Horace Walpole	S. Gwynn
Horace Walpole	Timothy Mowl
The Prime Minister of Taste	Morris Brownell
- A Portrait of Horace Walpole	
Horace Walpole – A Memoir	Austin Dobson
The Whig Supremacy 1714 – 1760	Basil Williams
The Great Swindle } South	Virginia Cowles
} Sea	
A Very English Deceit } Bubble	Malcolm Balen
Lord Hervey's Memoirs	Lord John Hervey
The Three Ladies Waldegrave	Violet Biddulph
and Their Mother	
Hanoverian London	George Rude
"Turnip" Townshend	Susanna Wade Martins
A Norfolk Gallery	R.W. Ketton – Cremer
The Log of a Rolling Stone	H.A Broome
British Prime Ministers	Douglas Hurd
- Sir Robert Walpole First Earl of Orford (1676-1745)	

The Creation of Houghton   John Cornforth
Sea Change (A Novel)   Robert Goddard

APPENDIX VIII

CHRIS BOXALL

Chris Boxall was born on 13th February 1946 in Peterborough. He was educated at St James' Primary Boys School and King Edward VII Grammar School in King's Lynn. He began working for West Norfolk Fertilisers before joining the Civil Service for almost 30 years, followed by 10 years with BBC Radio Norfolk.

An expert on Sir Robert Walpole, he now works during the summer months as a guide at Houghton Hall, Walpole's Norfolk home, describing it as "the best job I ever had!" He was also instrumental in persuading the King's Lynn and West Norfolk Borough Council to put up a sign in memory of Robert Walpole at the entrance of The Duke's Head Hotel on King's Lynn's Tuesday Market Place.

He is a film researcher and also studies military history, specialising in The Anglo-Zulu Wars (1879); D-Day and Operation Overlord (1944); The Battle of Waterloo (1815); The Somme (1916) and The Zeebrugge Raid (1918). He is also involved in Naval research, specialising in H.M.S. Hood (1916-1941); The Battle of the River Plate (1939); and H.M.S. Amethyst and the Yangtse Incident (1949).

The writer of several articles for newspapers and magazines, he is also the author of the books 'Raymond Rollett – The Forgotten Actor' and 'Old Sweats and Steelbacks'.

Recent research into the five Easton brothers of Olstead and Kilburn, N. Yorkshire – who served in the First World War – resulted in an article published in the 'Thirsk Weekly News'. In 2005 he wrote an article on the model soldier collection at Houghton Hall for 'Toy Soldier Collector' magazine. In 2006, he also updated the visitors' leaflet guide for the Cholmondeley collection of model soldiers at Houghton. He is also a member of the famous William Britain Model Soldiers Collectors' Club.

A member of the War Memorials Trust and the T.E. Lawrence Society, he lists his hobbies as visiting battlefields, military research, collecting model soldiers and military medals, cinema history, watching films and reading.

He is married to Heather, who is a Civil Servant, and they live in the NW Norfolk village of Dersingham with their faithful Norfolk Terrier, Scobie.

APPENDIX IX
ACKNOWLEDGEMENTS

I would like to take this opportunity of thanking all those people who have helped me in compiling this book for their time, knowledge, input and encouragement. In particular, special thanks are due to :-

Lord David Rocksavage, Marquess of Cholmondeley
Susan Cleaver – Administrator, Houghton Estate
David Yaxley – Houghton historian
John and Sheila Marchant – Head Guides, Houghton
Heather Boxall – For all her patience and input on all things technical
King's Lynn Press – For all their help and guidance
Vera and Derek Witt – For their help, advice and local historical knowledge
Bob and Connie Hood – Retired Houghton guides – For all their information
Dorothy Twist – Houghton guide and expert on William Kent
Dr Paul Richards – Historian and expert on the history of King's Lynn
Guides and Room Attendants, Houghton Hall – For their friendship and knowledge
And all those writers and historians who have provided me with details, quotations, inspiration and hours of enjoyable and fascinating reading. Many of them are listed in Appendix VII and, without them, this work would not have been possible.
And the memory of Percy Baldwin, former Administrator and Guide, Houghton Hall
and Eddie Pearson, former Head Guide, Houghton Hall.

I would like to thank Lord Cholmondeley, Susan Cleaver and the Houghton Estate for their kind permission to print those photographs which are the copyright of Houghton Hall. All other photographs are from the author's own collection.